POPULATION CONTROL POLICIES IN CHINA AND INDIA

This book comprehensively compares the development of population control policies in China and India, their implementations, and the population changes over the past seven decades.

Analyzing how populations have changed and affected socioeconomic development in the two societies, this book systematically compares China and India through social and cultural factors, including religion and traditional perspectives on population, ethnicity and language, social classes, family, social status and education of women, and government functions. A brief introduction discusses how China has developed into a highly homogenous society and how India has developed into a highly diversified nation in history, and the influence of other countries on these two societies. With empirical data, the book analyzes how population changes are strongly correlated with economic development in the two most populous societies. An insightful discussion of the population issues with a world perspective and historical understanding of China and India is also provided.

This book will be valuable reading to students and researchers interested in knowing more about the population control policies, population changes, and cultures and societies in China and India.

Gabe T. Wang is a professor of sociology at William Paterson University, USA. His research interests include population and development, juvenile delinquency, and cross-cultural comparisons. His publications include *China's Population: Problems, Thoughts and Policies* (1999) and *American Sociology and Socioeconomic Development in China* (2012).

Routledge Studies on Comparative Asian Politics

Books in this series will cover such areas as political institutions and systems, political economy, political culture, political thought, political psychology, public administration, law, and political histories of Asia. The studies may deal with Asia as a whole, a single country, or a group of countries in Asia. Those studies that have a clear comparative edge are especially welcome.

The Politics of Federalization in Myanmar
Dulyapak Preecharush

Democracy, State Capacity and the Governance of COVID-19 in Asia-Oceania
Aurel Croissant and Olli Hellmann

Population Control Policies in China and India
Comparisons with Social and Cultural Factors
Gabe T. Wang

For more information about this series, please visit: www.routledge.com/Routledge-Studies-on-Comparative-Asian-Politics/book-series/RSCAP

Population Control Policies in China and India

Comparisons with Social and Cultural Factors

Gabe T. Wang

Routledge
Taylor & Francis Group
LONDON AND NEW YORK

First published 2024
by Routledge
4 Park Square, Milton Park, Abingdon, Oxon OX14 4RN

and by Routledge
605 Third Avenue, New York, NY 10158

Routledge is an imprint of the Taylor & Francis Group, an informa business

Library of Congress Cataloging-in-Publication Data
Names: Wang, Gabe T., author.
Title: Population control policies in China and India / Gabe T. Wang.
Description: New York : Routledge, 2023. | Series: Routledge studies on comparative Asian politics | Includes bibliographical references and index.
Identifiers: LCCN 2023003848 (print) | LCCN 2023003849 (ebook) | ISBN 9781032309569 (hardback) | ISBN 9781032309552 (paperback) | ISBN 9781003307419 (ebook)
Subjects: LCSH: China—Population. | India—Population. | Birth control—China. | Birth control—India. | China—Social conditions. | India—Social conditions.
Classification: LCC HB3654.A3 W3456 2023 (print) | LCC HB3654.A3 (ebook) | DDC 304.6/0951—dc23/eng/20230309
LC record available at https://lccn.loc.gov/2023003848
LC ebook record available at https://lccn.loc.gov/2023003849

ISBN: 9781032309569 (hbk)
ISBN: 9781032309552 (pbk)
ISBN: 9781003307419 (ebk)

DOI: 10.4324/9781003307419

Typeset in Times New Roman
by Apex CoVantage, LLC

Contents

Figures

Tables

Acknowledgment

First, I would like to express my thanks to Dr. Zhenzhen Zheng at Chinese Social Sciences Academy who has helped me considerably with this book. Her comments and suggestions are extremely helpful.

Second, I would like to express my thanks to Dr. Robert Sauté who carefully edited my manuscript. His suggestions and comments are very helpful.

Finally, I would like to express my appreciation to my wife, Rong, for her love, support, and help with the book.

1 Population Control Policies in China and India

An Introduction

Significance of Understanding Population Control Policies in China and India

It is extremely important to understand the population control policies in China and India, the two most populous countries in the world. In 2022, China and India each had populations of about 1.4 billion (United Nations Department of Economic and Social Affairs/Population Division, 2022), meaning that each country has a billion more people than the United States, the third most populous country in the world. Together, China and India have about 2.8 billion people, which is more than the combined population of Europe, Latin America and the Caribbean, North America, and Oceania.

Since 1950, the world's population has increased dramatically from 2.5 billion to about eight billion. During this period, China and India have contributed 1.93 billion people to the world's population growth. To understand China and India is to understand more than a third of the world's population change in the past 72 years. By 2050, the combined population of China and India will be more than three billion. During the next 30 years, India will be the largest contributor to the world's population growth while China's population growth will have stabilized. "Throughout human history population has been synonymous with prosperity, stability, and security" (Livi-Bacci, 2012: 1). Population is the most fundamental information about a nation and its development.

During the past three centuries, many developed nations have experienced gradual demographic transitions from a period of high birth and death rates to a period of low birth and death rates. Demographic transitions in developed nations normally occur as a result of socioeconomic development, and transitions usually take a long time. For example, the population transition in England took more than 100 years between 1770 and 1870. In China and India, however, their demographic transitions have been affected by government's population control policies. As a result, demographic transitions in China and India have been considerably shortened, especially in China. This new phenomenon requires demographers to view population control policies in China and India in a new light.

People have worried about population growth for centuries. Some, like Malthus (1798), worried that when populations grew exponentially but food production

DOI: 10.4324/9781003307419-1

increased only arithmetically, people would starve. Others, like UNFPA Technical Division (2012), worried about the sustainability of the environment. Biologists Paul Ehrlich and Anne Ehrlich in their best-selling book (1968) even warned that rapid population growth in the world would be a "population bomb" soon to explode with dire consequences. Under such influences, China and India have adopted restrictive population control policies and implemented those policies with a great vigor, causing dramatic changes in their population growth. How have population control policies and their resulting changes affected these countries and the world? Should we be anxious about such population growth in an era when the world economy has developed more rapidly than global population growth?

After World War II, many developing countries have been urged by the Western nations to adopt policies to control their population growth so that their economies would be able to develop. Consequently, many developing countries implemented policies to curb their population growth. By the mid-1980s, 127 countries comprising 94% of the world's population officially supported family planning to some degree (Livi-Bacci, 2012). China's and India's population controls for the past seven decades have been most dramatic. How have their population control policies affected social and economic development?

To promote socioeconomic development, China and India adopted policies to curb population growth. Their enormous populations, however, have changed quite differently in the past seven decades. While China's percentage of the world's population decreased from 21.5% in 1950 to 18.1% in 2020, India's percentage of the world's population increased from 14.9% in 1950 to 17.9% in 2020. According to 2022 projections by the United Nations Department of Economic and Social Affairs/Population Division, India's population will overtake China's and become the most populous country in the world in 2023. Why did the populations change so differently in the two societies?

At the same time, rapid economic developments in China and India require a better understanding of the policies that shaped population changes and promoted socioeconomic development in the two nations. Between 1951 and 1989, the average gross domestic product (GDP) increased by 7.4% for China and 3.9% for India (Sun, 2007). During the past three decades, socioeconomic development in the two countries has accelerated. Since the 1990s, China's annual GDP grew about 9.9% and India's annual GDP grew about 6.5%. Although economic growth has slowed down in both countries in recent years, China's GDP increased by 6.9% and India's GDP grew by 6.7% in 2017.

In comparison, the United States' GDP increased by only 2.4% in 2017 (CIA, 2018). If calculated by purchasing power parity, China already has the world's largest economy with the United States and India ranked two and three, respectively. India's and China's economic predominance is not a new phenomenon. Based on the purchasing power parity, India's economy was about 22.6% of the world economy in 1700 and China's economy was about 32.4% of the world economy in 1820 (Ramesh, 2005). India's economy declined after the deindustrialization and cessation of various crafts industries under British rule after 1700 and China's economy declined after the defeat by the British navy in the First Opium War in

1840. They both fell behind when Western countries forged ahead after the Industrial Revolution.

India's independence in 1947 and the founding of the People's Republic of China (PRC) in 1949 marked the rising points of these two giant Asian countries. Both China and India have great potential in economic development. In 1980, China was the seventh and India was the 13th largest economy in the world. However, in 2019, China has the largest economy and India has the third largest economy in the world according to purchasing power parity (Silver, 2020).

If history repeats itself, which is now likely, China's and India's percentages of the world's total economy may reach the same historical heights they did during the 18th and 19th centuries. Then, China and India's combined percentage of the world economy could be half of the world economy in the future. Enormous populations and highly dynamic economic developments in China and India definitely require our attention and understanding.

Insufficient Understanding of Population Control Policies in China and India

China and India are the two most populous countries in the world today but hardly well understood. Scholars, politicians, and ordinary citizens have heard about population problems, population control policies, and policy implementations in China and India, and some have thought that population controls are necessary (Gu, 1995; Thomas, 1995; Brown, 1995; Nixon, 1988; Gupta, 2002). Others have claimed that their population controls have violated human rights (Aird, 1990; Follett, 2019). And still others thought that population control in China was unnecessary, the result of being misled by the West, or even a deadly error (Yu, 2012; Wang, Cai, and Gu, 2012; Wang et al., 2016).

Few people, however, have understood what the population control policies actually are in China and India or how population control policies have been implemented there. Even less understood is why their huge populations have changed so dramatically and differently. Similarly, few people have paid attention to the factors affecting the adoption and implementation of population control policies in China and India in the past seven decades.

Scholars have compared population control in China and India (Livi-Bacci, 2012; Li, 2004; Wang and Wu, 2003; Stolc, 2008), but most comparisons weigh specific aspects of population control, such as population growth rates, birth rates, or policy implementation differences. Few scholars have compared the Chinese and Indian population control policies and their implementations systematically. Even fewer have asked how cultural and social factors have influenced policies systematically.

Therefore, first, this book describes and summarizes the population control policies and their implementations in China and India. Second, it compares the population control policies and their implementations in the two societies. Third, it compares how population changes have affected economic developments in the two societies. Fourth and more important, the book compares the most fundamental social and cultural factors that have affected the adoption and implementation of population control policies in China and India. Lastly, the book summarizes and discusses the population control policies and relevant developmental aspects of China and India from world and historical perspectives.

Comparing China and India

This book's most important contribution is its comparative framework. Why compare population control policies and their implementations in China and India? Although they are different countries, they share many characteristics. Both civilizations have long histories and strong traditions. During the Industrial Revolution between the 18th and 19th centuries, Western nations forged ahead economically while China and India fell behind. While India became a British colony, China became a semi-colonial nation after being repeatedly invaded and defeated by foreign powers. To gain their independence, both countries struggled for more than a century. Finally, India gained its independence in 1947, and the PRC was founded in 1949.

When their new governments were established, both faced the same dilemma: They were desperately poor, and each had to bear the burden of a huge and rapidly increasing population. In 1950, China had a population of 544 million and India had a population of 376 million, the two largest populations in the world. At that time, both countries were extremely poor. Life expectancy was 35 years in China and 32 years in India (Sun, 2007).

When the PRC was founded and when India gained independence from Britain, the two societies stabilized. Land reforms, which were conducive to socioeconomic development, were carried out in both countries. However, when people had almost enough to eat and not enough money to be well-educated, the populations in both China and India began to grow explosively. In 1950, the average birth rate was 37 per thousand in China and 44.2 per thousand in India. Similarly, the average annual natural increase rate was 16 per thousand in China and 16.1 per thousand in India in 1951. Therefore, both countries wanted to develop their economy desperately, but both needed to control their enormous and rapidly growing population. Accordingly, India started its population control policies in 1952 and began to enforce mass sterilizations in the middle of the 1970s. Similarly, China began its population controls nationwide in the 1970s and started to implement its one-birth-per-couple policy in 1980.

Although China started its population control later than India, both perceived their huge populations as obstacles to badly needed socioeconomic development. Beginning in the 1950s, China and India adopted socialist or socialistic development strategies, and both made 5-year plans for their socioeconomic development. Later, China and India carried out economic reforms to introduce market mechanisms into their economy, China in the 1970s and India in the early 1990s. While trying to develop their economies, they continued their population controls.

However, China and India are different in many aspects. For example, China has a highly homogeneous society with more than 92% of its population speaking

Mandarin. India's highly diverse population speaks hundreds of languages. Within Chinese society, most are not religious. In contrast, almost everyone in India is religious. Since 1949, China's tightly organized society has been controlled by a strong central government that has significantly shaped its socioeconomic development. However, the highly diversified, loosely knit Indian society, with numerous differing religious beliefs, has been loosely controlled by a federal central government since its independence in 1947. The most obvious difference between the two nations is their political systems. Since the 1950s, many scholars and politicians all over the world have strenuously debated which of the countries would develop more rapidly. Although China has developed more rapidly in the past seven decades, many politicians and scholars believe that India has great potential to overtake China in terms of a near future increase in GDP growth, especially when China's population ages.

These historical and social conditions permit insightful comparisons of population control policies in China and India. They allow us to ask the following: How have their unique and different social structures, cultures, religions, family arrangements, women's status, and political systems affected population control policies and policy implementations? How have their population changes affected their socioeconomic developments in the past seven decades? What population and socioeconomic developments are likely in the future? In answering these fundamental questions, this book will make systematic comparisons of population control policies and their implementations. It will ask how different social and cultural factors affect policies and their implementations in the two societies. Such comparisons will enable us to understand China and India much better. They will also be valuable for those who are interested in socioeconomic development, politics, foreign relations, international trade, women's status, and the role of culture in social change. Those who are interested in the impact of China and India on the world will also substantially benefit.

Structure of the Book

This book consists of seven chapters. Chapter 1 provides a brief introduction to the study of population control policies in China and India and the significance of such a study. The chapter also explains why the two countries are comparable, why comparing them is badly needed, and what social and cultural factors may have affected the adoption and implementation of the two societies' population control policies.

Chapter 2 describes in detail the population control policies and their implementations in China. Specifically, it describes five periods of population control policy since the founding of the PRC in 1949. The five population control policy periods include the following: the limiting family planning period between 1949 and 1953, the fluctuating policy period between 1954 and 1970, the voluntary but effective family planning period between 1971 and 1979, the one-birth-per-couple policy period between 1980 and 2015, and the relaxing policy period since 2016. It also discusses how Mao Zedong, Deng Xiaoping, and Xi Jinping have influenced these policies. Then, the chapter analyzes how the different policies affected China's population growth. Lastly, the chapter offers a critical evaluation of the population control policies.

Similarly, Chapter 3 provides a detailed description of the population control policies in India. After a brief discussion of how Mahatma Gandhi and Jawaharlal Nehru influenced the population control policies in India, the chapter provides a detailed description of how population control policy developed through three periods. The first is a service-providing policy period between 1952 and 1961. During this period, the government population control policy started in a modest way and had little impact on the population growth in India. The second is an imperative and target-oriented policy period between 1962 and 1977 during which the government population control policy gradually tightened and forced sterilization was enforced. This period ended with the ruling party's defeat in the national election in 1977. The third is a voluntary policy period since April 1977 during which Indian population control policy gradually changed from an imperative and target-oriented policy to a comprehensive social development plan, although some targets have been maintained. The coercive measures have mostly been replaced by voluntary efforts, and population control has become indirect. With detailed population data, the chapter then summarizes and evaluates how the policies affected population growth and why economic development may bolster India's population control.

Chapter 4 systematically compares the population control policies and their implementations in China and India. It begins with a comparison of how the population perspectives of first-generation leaders affected the policies in China and India. It asks how the different population control policies started, tightened, and relaxed in the two societies. After a comparison of policy development, it explores how India's and China's policies have been implemented differently. China's specific population control policies, aimed at families, worked better than India's population control policies that aimed at generally reducing population growth. This chapter also shows how government population control policies differed in China and India. Finally, it delves into the consequences of the population control and shows how China's population has grown 3.4% more slowly while India's population has grown 3% faster than the world's population in the past seven decades. This difference of about 6.4% of the world's population could mean a difference of about 500 million people. Finally, the chapter points out the potential problems for China's effective population control and the continuous overpopulation issue in India.

Chapter 5 questions how population change has affected economic developments in the two societies. Having reviewed and summarized the literature on the relationship between population and economic development, this chapter briefly describes the most fundamental changes of the population and economic development in China and India. While China's per capita GDP increased from about $307 to about $10,580, India's per capita GDP grew from about $271 to about $1,880. Between 1980 and 2020, China's per capita GDP increased about 5.7 times that of India. Using empirical data, this chapter carefully analyzes correlations between population growth, total fertility rate, birth rate, natural increase rate, urbanization, total GDP, and per capita GDP. Empirical data analyses clearly indicate that population growth and urbanization are positively and strongly correlated to total GDP and per capita GDP in both countries. On the other hand, total fertility rate, birth rate, and natural increase rate are negatively correlated to total GDP and per capita GDP in the two societies. The findings of the chapter indicate that China has gone through its population transition much more rapidly than has India and therefore has developed its economy much more rapidly than has India.

Chapter 6 systematically compares seven major social and cultural factors that have affected population changes and made Chinese and Indian governments adopt different population control policies and their implementations. After a brief discussion of historical developments and external influences, the chapter explores the effects of religious and traditional differences on national values related to population, ethnicity and language, the social class, the family, the social status and education of women, and government in China and India. These factors closely relate to each other, and together, they have affected not only the population control policy but also the functioning of the two societies.

Chapter 7 concludes the book, summarizing and discussing population control policies in China and India on a macro level. It provides a fundamental understanding of not only population but also development issues. From a world's population perspective, the chapter discusses how world's population growth and Western perspectives have affected the two countries' population control policies and their implementations. Then, it also discusses the relationship between population and socioeconomic development in China and India. The author also provides perspectives on the population issues and socioeconomic development in the future. From a historical perspective, the final chapter evaluates population control policies and population changes in China and India and discusses how modern historical development has affected dramatic and similar changes in the evolution of China and India. The final discussions also point out the similarities between the two nations and differences in their recent development. Finally, the chapter raises reasonable expectations for China's and India's development.

References

Aird, John S. 1990. *Slaughter of the Innocents: Coercive Birth Control in China*. Washington, DC: The AEI Press.

Brown, L. 1995. *Who Will Feed China? Wake-up Call for a Small Planet*, Worldwatch Environmental Alert Series. New York, NY: W. W. Norton and Company.

CIA. 2018. "World Factbook. India, Economy". Retrieved on May 23, 2020 from www.cia.gov/library/publications/the-world-factbook/geos/in.html.

Ehrlich, Paul R. and Anne Ehrlich. 1968. *The Population Bomb*. New York, NY: Ballantine.

Follett, Chelsea. 2019. "The Cruel Truth About Population Control". *The National Interests*, June 13. Retrieved on March 17, 2023 from https://www.cato.org/commentary/cruel-truth-about-population-control.

Gu, J. T. 1995. "An Interview With Zhang Weiqing, the Vice Minister of the China State Family Planning Committee". *Market & Demographic Analysis*2(1): 4–7.

Gupta, Ashok. 2002. *A Billion Is Enough: India's Population Problem-A Way Out*. Chandigarh: Unistar Books Pvt, Ltd.
Li, Jianxin. 2004. "A Comparison of Population Power in the Future Between China and India". *Population Journal* 6.
Livi-Bacci, Massimo. 2012. *A Concise History of World Population*, 5th Edition. Malden, MA: John Wiley and Sons, Ltd.
Malthus, Thomas R. 1798 [1965]. *An Essay on Population*. New York, NY: Augustus Kelley.
Nixon, Richard. 1988. *1999: Victory Without War*. New York, NY: Simon and Schuster.
Ramesh, Jairam. 2005. *Making Sense of Chindia*. New Delhi: India Research Press.
Silver, Baleb. 2020. "The Top 20 Economies in the World: Ranking the Richest Countries in the World. Economy". *Investopedia*. Retrieved on May 25, 2020 from www.investopedia.com/insights/worlds-top-economies/#2-china.
Stolc, Phyllis E. W. 2008. "Seeking Zero Growth: Population Policy in China and India". *Graduate Journal of Asia-Pacific Studies* 6 (2): 10–32.
Sun, Peijun. 2007. *The Comparative Research on the Economic Development Between China and India*. Beijing: Economic Management Publisher.
Thomas, N. 1995. "The Ethics of Population Control in Rural China, 1979–92". *International Journal of Population Geography*1: 3–18.
UNFPA Technical Division. 2012. "Population Matters for Sustainable Development". Retrieved on May 18, 2020 from www.unfpa.org/public/cache/offonce/home/publications.
United Nations Department of Economic and Social Affairs/Population Division. 2022. "World Population Prospects 2022, Summary of Results". Retrieved on September 5, 2022 from www.un.org/development/desa/pd/sites/www.un.org.development.desa.pd/files/wpp2022_summary_of_results.pdf.
Wang, Dehua and Yang Wu. 2003. *The Dragon and the Elephant: A Comparison of the Rise of China and India During the 21st Century*. Shanghai: Shanghai Social Sciences Press.
Wang, Feng, Yong Cai and Baochang Gu. 2012. "Population, Policy, and Politics: How Will History Judge China's One-Child Policy?" *Population and Development Review* 38: 115–129.
Wang, Zhihe, Ming Yang, Jiaming Zhang, and Jiang Chang. 2016. "Ending an Era of Population Control in China: Was the One-Child Policy Ever Needed?" *American Journal of Economics & Sociology* 75: 929–979.
Yu, Fuxuan. 2012. *Big Country With an Empty Nest*. Beijing: Development Publisher of China.

2 Population Control Policies and Their Implementations in China[1]

Introduction

With strong and effective population control policies, China has substantially reduced its population growth. Over the last six decades, China's population growth has transitioned from a high birth rate and high death rate period to a low birth rate and low death rate period. As a result, China will no longer be the most populous country in the world in 2023 (United Nations Department of Economic and Social Affairs/Population Division, 2022). Although China's one-birth-per-couple policy is well-known, few are familiar with how China's population control policies and their implementations have changed since the founding of the People's Republic of China (PRC) in 1949. China's population control policies have affected not only population growth but also dramatic socioeconomic development in China.

Generally speaking, since the founding of the PRC, China's population control policies can be divided into five periods. In the first period, between 1949 and 1953, Chinese government policy sought to limit family planning through the use of contraceptives and abortion. During the second period from 1954 to 1970, the government gradually developed family planning programs. Program implementation, however, fluctuated repeatedly. A voluntary but effective family planning policy marked a third period between 1971 and 1979 when the government adopted a policy that strongly promoted "later marriage and birth, longer intervals between births, and fewer children" for each couple. The fourth period is between 1980 and 2015 during which the government implemented the well-known "one child" policy, which has decreased China's birth rate below the replacement level. Starting in 2016, the government has adopted a new two-children-per-couple policy.

This chapter provides a concise description of the population control policies and their implementations in each of these five periods, briefly discusses how dominant Chinese leaders have influenced the policy adoption, and evaluates and discusses the population control policies and their implementations, which should increase our understanding of the policies and the functioning of Chinese society. With China's increasing impact on the world, our understanding of how the Chinese government adopts population control policies should be significant.

DOI: 10.4324/9781003307419-2

China's Five Periods of Population Control Policies and Their Implementations

1. The Limiting Family Planning Period Between 1949 and 1953

Immediately after the founding of the PRC in 1949, population was not perceived as a problem, and the Chinese government had no specific nationwide policy toward population growth. However, the government limited family planning, the use of contraceptives, and abortion. On December 31, 1952, the Cultural and Educational Committee of the State Council of China ratified the "Temporary Regulations on Limiting Family Planning and Abortion." According to the proposed regulations, government employees who had abortions without permission and their providers would be punished. The government also banned the import of contraceptives (Tian, 2009). The adoption of the policy was influenced partly by the Soviet Union, traditional family values, and the long period of wars in China.

In January 1953, the government proposed and tested a policy prohibiting birth control and abortion in five provinces in Northern China. Half a year later, however, the government realized that the policy was unpopular. Many women complained that too many children made their lives more difficult, and they wanted to practice birth control. In fact, some women illegally practiced birth control, and illegal abortions occurred frequently. Illegal birth control and abortions were harmful to women's health, sometimes even endangering their lives.

Having investigated existing problems of illegal birth control and abortion, the Health Ministry reported to the Government Administration Council in August 1953 that the proposed policy was not appropriate for those who had had several children. The policy's many negative consequences included endangering women's lives. Accordingly, the Health Ministry suggested to the central government that within 3 to 5 years, under the supervision of the Health Care Administration, birth control devices should be produced, sold, and used by the public. It also suggested that the government disseminate birth control information within appropriate groups of people and loosen the restriction on abortion.

After the establishment of the PRC in 1949, Chinese society stabilized, peace was restored, economic development recovered and accelerated, and health care improved substantially. Although government policies that limited the use of family planning and abortion had little effect on Chinese society, China's population started to grow rapidly. As a result, its birth rate slightly increased from 36 per thousand in 1949 to 37 per thousand in 1953 while the death rate decreased from 20 per thousand in 1949 to 14 per thousand in 1953. During the same period, China's natural increase rate increased from about 16 to 23 per thousand (see Table 2.1), although China's total fertility remained at about six (births per woman). At that time, the Chinese government did not realize that its huge population would grow much more rapidly than it had expected.

2. The Fluctuating Policy Period Between 1954 and 1970

The second period between 1954 and 1970 saw a gradual development of China's population control policy from limiting birth control to strongly advocating family

Table 2.1 China's Total Population, Total Fertility, Birth Rate, Death Rate, Natural Increase Rate, and Urbanization Percentage (1950–2020)

Year	*Population (Thousands)*	*Total Fertility*	*Birth Rate (per 1000)*	*Death Rate (Per 1000)*	*Natural Increase Rate (per 1000)*	*Urbanization Percentage*
1950	551,960	6.49	37.00	18.00	19.00	11.2
1951	563,000	6.56	37.80	17.80	20.00	11.8
1952	574,820	6.24	37.00	17.00	20.00	
1953	587,960	6.11	37.00	14.00	23.00	
1954	602,660	6.98	37.97	13.18	24.79	
1955	614,650	5.86	32.60	12.28	20.32	13.5
1956	628,280	5.73	31.90	11.40	20.50	
1957	646,530	5.61	34.03	10.80	23.23	
1958	659,940	5.48	29.22	11.98	17.24	
1959	672,070	5.61	24.78	14.59	10.19	
1960	662,070	5.75	20.86	25.43	−4.57	19.8
1961	658,590	5.88	18.02	14.24	3.78	
1962	672,950	6.02	37.01	10.02	26.99	
1963	691,720	6.15	43.37	10.04	33.33	
1964	704,990	6.18	39.14	11.50	27.64	
1965	725,380	6.21	37.88	9.50	28.38	18.0
1966	745,420	6.24	35.05	8.83	26.22	
1967	763,680	6.27	33.96	8.43	25.53	
1968	785,340	6.30	35.59	8.21	27.38	
1969	806,710	6.01	34.11	8.03	26.08	
1970	829,920	5.72	33.43	7.60	25.83	17.4
1971	852,290	5.43	30.65	7.32	23.33	17.3
1972	871,770	5.14	29.77	7.61	22.16	17.1
1973	892,110	4.85	27.93	7.04	20.89	17.2
1974	908,590	4.48	24.82	7.34	17.48	17.2
1975	924,200	4.14	23.01	7.32	15.69	17.3
1976	937,170	3.75	19.91	7.25	12.66	17.4
1977	949,740	3.38	18.93	6.87	12.06	17.6
1978	962,590	3.01	18.25	6.25	12.00	17.9
1979	975,420	2.91	17.82	6.21	11.61	19.0
1980	987,050	2.81	18.21	6.34	11.87	20.0
1981	1,000,720	2.72	20.91	6.36	14.55	20.2
1982	1,016,540	2.62	22.28	6.60	15.68	21.1
1983	1,030,080	2.52	21.19	6.90	13.29	21.6
1984	1,043,570	2.56	19.90	6.82	13.08	23.0
1985	1,058,510	2.60	21.04	6.78	14.26	23.7
1986	1,075,070	2.65	22.43	6.86	15.57	24.5
1987	1,093,000	2.69	23.33	6.72	16.61	25.3
1988	1,110,260	2.73	22.37	6.64	15.73	25.8
1989	1,127,040	2.55	21.58	6.54	15.04	26.2
1990	1,143,330	2.37	21.06	6.67	14.39	26.4
1991	1,158,230	2.19	19.68	6.70	12.98	26.9
1992	1,171,710	2.01	18.24	6.64	11.60	27.5
1993	1,185,170	1.83	18.09	6.64	11.45	28.0

(Continued)

Table 2.1 (Continued)

Year	*Population (Thousands)*	*Total Fertility*	*Birth Rate (per 1000)*	*Death Rate (Per 1000)*	*Natural Increase Rate (per 1000)*	*Urbanization Percentage*
1994	1,198,500	1.79	17.70	6.49	11.21	28.5
1995	1,211,210	1.75	17.12	6.57	10.55	29.0
1996	1,223,890	1.70	16.98	6.56	10.42	30.5
1997	1,236,260	1.66	16.57	6.51	10.06	31.9
1998	1,247,610	1.62	15.64	6.50	9.14	33.4
1999	1,257,860	1.62	14.64	6.46	8.18	34.8
2000	1,267,430	1.62	14.03	6.45	7.58	36.2
2001	1,276,270	1.61	13.38	6.43	6.95	37.7
2002	1,285,430	1.61	12.86	6.41	6.45	39.1
2003	1,292,270	1.61	12.41	6.40	6.01	40.5
2004	1,299,880	1.61	12.29	6.42	5.87	41.8
2005	1,307,560	1.61	12.40	6.51	5.89	43.0
2006	1,314,480	1.62	12.09	6.81	5.28	44.3
2007	1,321,290	1.62	12.10	6.93	5.17	45.9
2008	1,328,020	1.62	12.14	7.06	5.08	47.0
2009	1,334,500	1.62	11.95	7.08	4.87	48.3
2010	1,340,910	1.63	11.90	7.11	4.79	50.0
2011	1,349,160	1.63	13.27	7.14	6.13	51.8
2012	1,359,220	1.64	14.57	7.13	7.43	53.1
2013	1,367,260	1.64	13.03	7.13	5.90	54.5
2014	1,376,460	1.65	13.83	7.12	6.71	55.8
2015	1,383,260	1.66	11.99	7.07	4.93	57.3
2016	1,392,320	1.67	13.57	7.04	6.53	58.8
2017	1,400,110	1.68	12.64	7.06	5.58	60.2
2018	1,405,410	1.69	10.86	7.08	3.78	61.5
2019	1,410,080	1.69	10.41	7.09	3.32	62.7
2020	1,412,120	1.70	8.52	7.07	1.45	63.9

Sources:

1. Data between 1950 and 1979 were according to the data provided by Yao and Yin (1994) Basic Data of China's Population. Population Press of China, Beijing. P. 9.
2. Data between 1980 and 2000 were according to the National Bureau of Statistics of China (2021), National Data, Population. Retrieved on September 21, 2022, at www.stats.gov.cn/tjsj/ndsj/2021/indexch.htm.
3. Total fertility was according to the Macrotrends (2021) data retrieved on April 7, 2021, from www.macrotrends.net/countries/CHN/china/population

planning. On May 27, 1954, the vice-chair of the National Woman's Association, Deng Yinchao sent a letter to the then Vice Premier Deng Xiaoping. The letter stated that limiting birth control and abortion was inappropriate and that many women cadres complained about the policy. Lacking knowledge and suitable contraceptives forced many women to utilize unhealthy and inappropriate measures of birth control, making it necessary to request that the government adopt proper measures to address the problem. In her letter, Deng Yinchao also mentioned that the birth rate in China was high and that it was necessary to publicize birth control and allow family planning first among government employees. On the following day, Deng Xiaoping commented on Deng Yinchao's letter agreeing that birth control was absolutely necessary and beneficial to the country. At the same time, Deng Xiaoping instructed the Health Ministry to take measures to deal with the problem (Zhou, 1986).

Consequently, the idea of birth control became acceptable to the Chinese government, mostly for the sake of women's health. In July 1954, the Government Administration Council approved and promulgated birth control and abortion regulations drafted by the Health Ministry. This document virtually revoked the previously proposed policy limiting birth control and abortion. However, this did not mean that the government intended to control population growth in China.

Having established social order and restored economic development, the Chinese government began to pay attention to population in 1953 and decided to conduct a census in the same year. The first census carried out between 1953 and 1954 revealed that China's population was over 600 million and growing by 2 percent yearly. A few government officials then started to realize the necessity of population control for China. In September 1954, at the First National People's Congress, Shao Lizi, a representative of the People's Congress, mildly rebutted Chairman Mao Zedong's statement that a large population was a good thing. Mao made the statement in an article rebutting Dean Acheson's letter to US President Harry Truman. Shao argued that it was a delightful thing to have a large population; however, it seemed that there should be limitations while facing many difficulties. He also suggested that the government should publicize birth control information and provide people with guidance and birth control devices.

As a result, the Health Ministry issued a bulletin on improving birth control and abortion on September 10, 1954. It instructed government organizations not to restrict birth control, but to provide guidance to anyone who needed birth control and allow all types of contraceptives to be sold on the market. It also directed relevant organizations to loosen their control over abortion (Zhou, 1986). The bulletin pointed out that it was inappropriate to publicize birth control. A woman could have an abortion only when she and her husband agreed and it was approved by a doctor and her work organization. Sterilization was limited to those who had already given six births or those whose health was endangered by continuous pregnancy. Similarly, a woman's sterilization could only be performed when husband and wife agreed, and it was approved by a doctor and her work organization (Jiang and Zhang, 1997). The government was not yet ready for population control, and birth control, abortion, and sterilization were not encouraged but only for the sake of a woman's health.

On November 27, 1954, President Liu Shaoqi convened a forum on birth control, at which he declared that the Communist Party endorsed birth control and it should be promoted instead of opposed (Liu, 1984). Government leaders had become convinced that reducing population growth and birth control were necessary to improve the quality of people's lives. Two months later, on January 31, 1955, the Health Ministry sent a report on birth control to the Central Committee of the Chinese Communist Party (CCP) stating that China had a population of more than 600 million, and rapid population growth might cause problems for the country as well as individual families. Birth control was the democratic right of each male and female citizen; therefore, the government should not deprive citizens of this right.

In March 1955, the Central Committee of the CCP ratified the report and issued a directive indicating that birth control was an important policy related to people's lives. It should be appropriately practiced for the interests of the country, individual families, and the younger generation. The instruction also required all echelons of the Communist Party to appropriately publicize the policy throughout the country except in minority-inhabited areas, for the minority population was usually small and has privileges in China. The central government's approval of the Health Ministry report was made, however, mostly out of consideration for women and children's health rather than population control.

The government formally advocated family planning in 1956 when the National Agricultural Development Outline stated that in all densely populated areas, except those inhabited by minorities, birth control should be advocated and publicized. In September 1956, at the Eighth National Congress of the CCP, birth control policy first became part of the Second Five-Year Plan of National Economic Development. The policy, however, was swept aside when the Great Leap Forward campaign started in 1957. This campaign attempted to utilize a large number of people in rural areas to accelerate economic development.

Nevertheless, the birth control policy was reaffirmed in 1962 after China's Great Leap Forward campaign failed and the country suffered a serious famine between 1960 and 1961. On December 18, 1962, the Central Committee and the State Council jointly issued A Directive on Sincerely Advocating Family Planning. The Directive clearly stated that advocating family planning in urban and densely populated rural areas, controlling the natural population increase rate appropriately, and gradually changing unplanned births into planned births were to be established policies in China's socialist construction. In a speech before the Standing Committee of the People's Congress in 1963, Premier Zhou Enlai also stated that China must adopt effective policies and take effective steps to practice family planning. He pointed out that family planning included both later marriage and birth control (Jiang and Zhang, 1997).

The birth control policy became substantiated in 1964 when the Family Planning Office of the State Council was set up to take charge of matters pertaining to family planning. Corresponding offices were set up in provinces, cities, and minority autonomous regions throughout the country. These newly established organizations started distributing contraceptives throughout the nation. Both Shanghai Municipality and Wendeng County in Shandong Province started to require married couples to put off pregnancy until a late date, have fewer children, and wait longer intervals between births. This family planning program experimented locally before becoming a nationwide policy. Implementation of the birth control policy, however, was again interrupted, this time by the Cultural Revolution, which started in 1966.

Although the government gradually developed and tested a population control policy in some areas during this period, the policy was never a nationwide policy and was never implemented nationwide. As a result, China's total fertility decreased slightly from 6.28 in 1954 to 5.81 in 1970. During the same period, China's birth rate slightly reduced from about 37.97 per thousand in 1954 to 33.43 per thousand in 1970 while the death rate fell almost by half from 13.18 per thousand in 1954 to about 7.60 per thousand in 1970. Similarly, China's natural increase rate increased from 24.78 per thousand in 1954 to about 25.83 per thousand in 1970. China's percentage of the world's total population remained, however, around 22% between 1950 and 1970 (Wang, 2018), which may indicate that China's population was growing at an average level of the world during the period between 1950 and 1970.

3. The Voluntary but Effective Family Planning Period Between 1971 and 1979

Between 1949 and 1970, people's lives and health care were substantially improved. As a result, the death rate in China declined from 20 per thousand in 1949 to 7.6 per thousand in 1970. Life expectancy increased from 44.6 years in 1949 to 64.6 years in 1970. The total population also increased from about 541,670,000 in 1949 to about 829,920,000 in 1970, which put pressure on education, employment, housing, and capital accumulation (China Development Research Foundation, 2012).

China's earnest effort to control its population growth actually began in 1971 when Mao Zedong paid attention to the looming population problem and issued an instruction that population growth must be brought under control. Chairman of the CCP until he passed away in 1976, Mao had played an extraordinary role in the Chinese revolution before and after the Party came to power in 1949. He possessed extraordinary prestige and power in China. During the early 1970s, Mao's works were regarded as a bible to be repeatedly studied, recited, and followed, and his instructions were carried out effectively throughout the whole nation, from large cities to small villages.

After Mao's instructions, the Chinese government asked single people across the country to put off marriage and bearing children. Generally, males were asked to marry at the age of 25 and females at 23. For married couples, the government asked couples to stretch the interval between births, usually to more than 3 years between births. At the same time, married couples were asked to have fewer children, usually only two. The local government population control policy in Shanghai Municipality and Wendeng County in Shandong Province was actually applied nationwide in 1973. Under the planned economy or collective economic system, government influence reached every neighborhood in urban areas and every village in the countryside. As a result, most Chinese accepted the policy and began family planning right away.

In addition to Mao's directives, the State Council also issued Document Number 51, which proposed China's goals for family planning during the period of the Fourth Five-Year Plan for National Economic Development between 1971 and 1975. The document stated that China must reduce natural population increases to about 1 percent in urban areas and 1.5 percent in rural areas and maintain the natural increase rate in those areas where it was already low. Except for those sparsely populated and minority-inhabited areas, the population control policy should be implemented. The population control policy, though, lacked coercive enforcement measures.

In 1973, population control became a national policy under the direction of the National Report Conference on Family Planning. Accordingly, the State Council reestablished the Leading Group for Family Planning and nominated Hua Guofeng who later became the premier of the State Council. When Vice Premier Chen Muhua became the head of the Leading Group in 1978, she immediately called a group meeting and the Leading Group summarized previous family planning experiences from across the nation and developed a new family planning strategy that included the following: requesting the party secretary at all government levels take leadership in family planning, requiring all Party members to set a good example, be involved in family planning promotion through propaganda and education, strengthen scientific research in family planning, improve family planning technologies and devices, put effective measures into practice, mobilize mass participation, and adhere to family planning throughout society (Tian, 2009). With a national population control policy, specific goals, and comprehensive implementation strategies, China's birth rate dropped considerably.

In 1978, the first session of the Fifth National People's Congress ratified the new constitution, which explicitly stipulated that the state advocate and encourage family planning. This was the first time since 1949 that family planning was established in law and became a fundamental duty of all citizens. In his report to the Congress, the then Premier Hua Guofeng stated as follows:

> Family planning is a very significant matter. Controlling population growth according to plan is conducive to the planned development of the national economy and beneficial to the health of mother and child. It also benefits the production and individuals' work and study. We must continue to give it a serious attention and strive to lower the annual rate of growth of China's population to less than one percent within three years.
>
> (1978: 29)

Although the population control in this period was voluntary, it was effective because the government strongly controlled Chinese society, and people much more willingly complied with government policy. What enabled the government to implement population control was state-owned or collective economic organizations in both urban and rural areas. When the economy was strictly under the government's aegis, family planning was easily implemented, a two-children-per-couple social norm was quickly formed, and China's birth rate declined right away. In fact, China's birth rate reduced from 30.65 per thousand in 1971 to 17.82 per thousand in 1979. Similarly, the annual population increase rate also declined from 23.33 per thousand in 1971 to 11.61 per thousand in 1979 (see Table 2.1). During the same period, the total fertility rate (TFR) also considerably reduced from 5.44 to 2.75 (Yao and Yin, 1994). However, China's percentage of the world's population remained at about 22%, which indicates that the world's population growth during the 1970s decreased considerably as well.

4. The One-Birth-Per-Couple Policy Period Between 1980 and 2015

After 1978, the Chinese government's attention switched exclusively to economic development. In 1979, during the Second Session of the Fifth National People's Congress, the central government and the congress lawmakers deem the one-birth-per-couple policy was necessary in light of China's large population base, its youthful age structure, rapid growth, and long baby boom in the 1960s. The strategic goal of the policy was to keep China's population under 1.2 billion and quadruple China's GNP by the year 2000. Accordingly, China's population control became much more restrictive.

The one-birth-per-couple policy in China, more commonly but inaccurately known as the one-child policy, means that each couple is restricted to only one birth. There is always the possibility of twins or triplets, for example. The one-birth-per-couple policy was considered necessary by demographers and policy makers who strongly believed that only a very restrictive policy could upset the looming baby boom that would start in the 1980s. At the same time, the Chinese government determined to carry out population control firmly and vigorously, which it considered essential for China's development. For example, in March 1979, in his speech on maintaining the four basic principles for China's development, the late Chinese leader Deng Xiaoping pointed out that the Chinese must understand two fundamental characteristics of China: First, the country is poor, and second, it has a large population and little tillable land. At that time, the population was more than 900 million with about 80 percent farmers. A large population has advantages and disadvantages. While production is still underdeveloped, food, education, and employment are all serious problems. Therefore, China must vigorously pursue family planning. Even if the population stops growing, China would still have an overpopulation problem (Deng, 1983).

Since the economic reforms, which started in the late 1970s, the government has loosened control on almost all aspects of people's activities in the country. Population control, however, was an exception, and the government maintained restrictive controls until 2015. In 1980, when inspecting Sichuan Province, Deng Xiaoping also emphasized that the government had to adhere to the policy that each couple could have only one birth, and the government would not make concessions on this policy. If the government did so, there would be no hope to realize the four modernizations (Zhou, 1986). Obviously, overpopulation was perceived as a major obstacle to China's development, and population control policy has become a fundamental part of China's developmental strategy.

From March to May in 1980, the Central Committee of the CCP held five forums to discuss the one-birth-per-couple policy. More than 60 government officials from different departments—including natural scientists from hospitals and universities and social scientists from different disciplines—participated in the forum discussions that considered possible consequences and side effects of the policy. The forums recommended the one-birth-per-couple policy to the Chinese government, proposing to reward those who follow the policy and have only one birth and punish those who have more than two births in rural areas (Tian, 2009).

On September 7, 1980, at the Third Session of the Fifth People's Congress of China, Premier Hua Guofeng announced that China would adopt a one-birth-per-couple policy. On September 25, the Central Committee issued a public letter to all the members of the Party and the Communist League expounding on population issues in China and advocating the one-birth-per-couple policy. On February 9, 1982, the Central Committee and the State Council issued a further directive on family planning that required government employees, officials, and urban residents to have only one birth. It also advocated that rural residents follow the policy, but minorities were allowed more than one birth (China Development Research Foundation, 2012).

When the one-birth-per-couple policy became effective, the actual practice of population control was more restrictive in cities and densely populated rural areas than the government has been admitted, for second births were rarely permitted in those areas; the family planning norms the People's Congress advocated had practically become law. In implementing the policy, administrative directives were not simply advocated but actually enforced. In 1982 in densely populated areas, sterilization was mandatory for many Han couples, the majority Chinese group, with two or more children. In 1983, abortion, sometimes by coercion, was widely practiced for unauthorized births.

During the early 1980s and 1990s, married couples were monitored regularly by village, neighborhood, or workplace family planning personnel to ensure compliance with the regulations. Before conceiving a baby, couples were expected to secure official permission so that childbirth would be in accordance with plan. In 1988, in cities 94 percent of births were preapproved, 57 percent in towns, and 52 percent in the rural areas (Sanderson and Tan, 1995). Although the central government did not allow coercive means in implementing the population control policy, the practice of evaluating local government adherence to family planning directives encouraged the use of coercion to enforce the policy at the grassroots level.

After economic reform was in full swing in the early 1980s, the central government firmly stressed the importance of population control and requested all echelons of the government enforce the restrictive policy. However, when the People's Communes were disbanded and the collective economy substantially disintegrated, the labor force became more important for privatized economic activities. As a result, population control policy implementation faced increased resistance, especially in rural areas. At the same time, with economic reforms considerably reducing the effectiveness of government organizations, especially in rural areas, family planning cadres found that individuals no longer took government policy seriously, and administrative directives became less powerful.

Family planning cadres often resorted to pressure or coercive measures to implement the more restrictive but less popular one-birth-per-couple policy. Female infanticide, though not as widely practiced as some Western news media portrayed, was indeed reported in varied areas. As a result, the policy was perceived as too restrictive by many Chinese, although they endorsed population control in principle and were ready to make sacrifices for development. Families, when they were asked to reduce the number of children they planned to have from four or five to two, made the sacrifice. However, asking them to reduce the number of children to one was unacceptable.

When families reported complaints about coercion, the government tried to maintain the population control policy but urged family planning cadres to refrain from coercive measures. It strongly requested that lower-level family planning cadres rely on persuasion and educational methods to conduct their work. In 1984, the government even slightly relaxed the policy and permitted more couples to have a second birth. More specifically, those couples whose first child was a female were allowed to have a second birth. Minorities were allowed to have two or three children while those who lived in large-sized and medium-sized cities were restricted to one birth. This small relaxation, however, quickly sent the national birth rate from 19.90 per thousand in 1984 to 23.33 per thousand in 1987, prompting the government to tighten population control again. As a result, pressure on those who wanted to have the second or third birth increased, and some women were forced to have an intrauterine contraceptive device inserted or undergo an abortion.

Since the birth rate in China increased during the mid-1980s, the CCP Central Committee and the State Council jointly issued a policy statement in 1991 calling for improving family planning and more rigorous control of population growth. The statement argued that China faced the urgent task of controlling population growth by diligently implementing current family planning policy. The statement required all government levels to place population control high on their agenda and called on members of the Party, soldiers, and government employees to take the lead in abiding by and carrying out the family planning policy (China Daily, 1991). As a result, the birth rate decreased below the replacement level in the early 1990s.

In the 1990s, the Chinese government continued its restrictive population control policy but relied more and more on economic measures to enforce the policy. The new mechanisms included combining family planning with economic development, aid to improve farmers' lives, and the establishment of civilized and happy families. Gradually, the one-birth-per-couple policy became widely accepted in the urban areas, and many people in these areas took the policy for granted. Implementation of the policy in rural areas, however, remained the most challenging job for rural family planning cadres. Fines that were mostly in proportion to family incomes were widely used to enforce the policy. When family planning programs did not work well, the rapidly developing economy did. With the help of the rapid socioeconomic development and urbanization, birth rates continued to drop below the replacement level in the 1990s.

Between 2000 and 2015, China continued its one-birth-per-couple policy. In December 2001, the Chinese government adopted a Population and Family Planning Law that became effective on September 1, 2002. For the first time in history, China's population control policy was escalated to the level of law. During the following years, the Chinese government leaders continued to emphasize the importance of population control, although the rate of population increase fell substantially. Scholars believe that this was because the government was misinformed by demographers who did not believe that China's population growth was reduced as much as the population census had indicated (Yi, 2012).

On December 17, 2006, the government published Enforcing Population Control and Family Planning Tasks and Uniformly Solve the Population Problem. The decision called on government officials to try their best to stabilize the low birth rate, maintain the fundamental policy of family planning, and continue population control. The decision also called on Party and government leaders to enforce population control without hesitation. However, in 2013 after Xi Jinping came to power, the government decided to merge the Family Planning Commission into the new Public Health and Family Planning Commission, which deemphasized the exclusive population control function of the commission and signaled a revision of the population control policy in the near future.

During this period, China's population control policy was known as the one-child policy, but the proposed policies and those actually implemented went beyond the country's usual population programs. The policy also sought to control population distribution, that is, migration in addition to limiting population growth.

The new policy included four parts. The first pertained to late marriage. According to the Marriage Law adopted by the third session of the Fifth People's Congress on September 15, 1980, the minimum permissible age for marriage was 20 for women and 22 for men. The revised policy called for a 3-year delay; women and men were advised to get married at the ages of 23 and 25. Part two was late childbearing, which meant that women were asked to bear their first child between 24 and 30 years of age. The third factor called for fewer children. Couples were expected to have only one birth; it looked to strictly control second births and resolutely prevent third births. Families that faced special difficulties were exempt from this restriction. Special difficulties included the following: (1) families that had a physically or mentally handicapped child, (2) couples that had remarried and one of the remarried partners had never had a child, (3) both of a newly married couple were single children, (4) when a couple in which the male member had brothers who were unable to have children, (5) a male who married into a family with no male children, (6) families in rural areas that had only one female child, (7) disabled veterans, (8) families that had adopted a child before but now were able to give birth to a child, (9) families in which both husband and wife returned to China from overseas, and (10) families that lived in remote mountainous or coastal areas (Tian, 2009). The fourth factor prohibited close kin and persons with congenital and genetic diseases from getting married so their child will be in good health. At the same time, good medical care was available for both pregnant women and newly born babies. Because of these comprehensive considerations of the social reality, China's population control policies were implemented more effectively.

In actual implementation, the population control policy was carefully tailored to meet the practical living needs of people in different regions of the country (Encyclopedia, 2020). For those who lived in areas that were densely populated but lacked arable land, population growth was controlled restrictively; for those who lived in sparsely populated areas, population control was less restrictive; and for those minorities that had a small population that grew slowly, population growth was encouraged.

During this period, China implemented its most restrictive population control policy, and its birth rate further declined from 18.21 per thousand in 1980 to 12.07 per thousand in 2015. During the same period, the natural increase rate further reduced from 11.87 per thousand in 1980 to 4.96 per thousand in 2015 (see Table 2.1). The TFR in China was also lowered from 2.24 children per woman in 1980 to 1.7 in 2015. At the same time, China's percentage of the world's population fell from about 22% in 1980 to about 19% in 2015, indicating substantial success in population control.

5. The Relaxing Policy Period Since 2016

The one-birth-per-couple policy was originally adopted for 30 years and was supposed to end by 2010. Within 30 years, China's birth rate reduced from 18.21 per thousand in 1980 to 11.90 per thousand in 2010. The annual population increase rate also declined from 11.87 per thousand in 1980 to 4.79 per thousand in 2010 (see Table 2.1). During the same period, the percentage of the population under 15 years old declined from 33.59% to 16.60% (China Development Research Foundation, 2012). Obviously, the population increase rate has fallen, the population age and gender structures have changed, and an adjustment of the population control policy seems necessary.

Many scholars and government officials, however, strongly believed that the national census taken in 2010 underreported the real birth numbers and still worried that a relaxation of the one-birth-per-couple policy would cause another baby boom, although the total birth rate in China has been below the replacement level, 2.1 children per woman, since the 1990s. Nevertheless, empirical research has indicated that another baby boom was unlikely. Most married women are unlikely to have a second child even if the policy would allow more children (Liu, 2013a; Zheng, 2013; Bai, 2014).

On the other hand, other scholars (He, 2013; Liu, 2013b; Yi, 2012) have challenged the prevailing perspectives on population change and population control policies in China, partly due to China's declining birth rate to below the replacement level since the early 1990s. These scholars have systematically challenged the accuracy of the population data compiled by the dominant demographers, their predictions of population growth, the perspectives based on their data, and consequently, the one-birth-per-couple policy.

Although they are heterodox scholars, they have affected how people think of the population problem and Chinese policy. At the same time, researchers in organizations such as the China Development Research Foundation (2012) have pointed out that China's population has already fundamentally changed. Large-scale industrialization and urbanization have reduced China's birth rate. Yet the imbalance of gender and aging in the Chinese population has posed new challenges. Each of these arguments requires an adjustment of the one-birth-per-couple policy.

At the Fifth Plenary Session of the 18th Congress of the CCP held in October 2015, the Central Committee of the CCP adopted a new policy to allow married couples to have two children to promote balanced population growth. Although the Committee reaffirmed its fundamental policy to control China's population growth, it wanted to improve reproductive health and childcare, help families that practiced family planning but now have difficulties, and pay attention to family wellbeing (Xin Hua News Website, 2016). The Standing Committee of the Chinese People's Congress approved the Revision of the Law on Population and Family Planning in December 2015, and the new law became effective on January 1, 2016.

Later, the Central Committee and the State Council of China published a Decision on the Implementation of the Two-Children-Per-Couple Policy Nationwide and the Reformation and Improvement of the Management and Services of Family Planning on December 31, 2015. The Decision indicated that China's population control had already achieved great success, and China's population had substantially changed; therefore, a new two-children-per-couple policy was more appropriate for the nation. The new policy may also improve the structure of the Chinese population, increase the labor force, reduce the pressure on an aging population, and, therefore, be conducive to China's healthy socioeconomic development (Xin Hua News Website, 2016).

Although the new policy became effective on January 1, 2016, it has not significantly changed China's population growth since its implementation. During the past few years, China's birth rate has continued to decrease from 12.95 per thousand in 2016 to 10.48 per thousand in 2019. The natural increase rate continues to decrease from 5.86 per thousand in 2016 to 3.34 per thousand in 2019 (see Table 2.1). Since 2016, the TFR remains at 1.7 children per woman, below the replacement level of 2.1.

When more than 60% of China's population live in urban areas, when woman's education has been substantially improved and employment has been extensive, and when the cost of raising a child has substantially increased, the new Two-Children-Per-Couple Policy proved ineffective in changing either the growth rate or the gender and age structures of the Chinese population. The new policy is unlikely to improve the structure of the Chinese population or to alleviate the social problems caused by an aging population significantly.

Obviously, China needs to take greater steps in revising its population control policy if the government wants to improve the population structure in Chinese society. Recently, some scholars and politicians in China have proposed to allow couples to have three children instead of two. Scholars like Professor Song Jian at Renmin University in Beijing have suggested that China needs to boost its willingness to have children and make people feel that having children or forming a family is attractive (Stachel, 2023).

After China's Seventh National Census, completed in 2020, it was obvious that China's fertility rate was still falling, the aged population was increasing rapidly, the TFR has been below the replacement level for more than two decades already, and China's total population would be decreasing. The National People's Congress responded by amending the family planning law. Accordingly, the Central

Committee of the CCP and the State Council unveiled the Decision on Optimizing the Family Planning Policy to Promote the Long-Term and Balanced Development of the Population on June 26, 2021. This decision proclaimed a new Three-Children-Per-Couple Policy (Xinhua, 2021). It also rolled out supporting measures, ranging from tax breaks to more nurseries and flexible work leave for married couples to encourage births. Local governments quickly adopted new preferential supporting policies for couples who wanted to have three children, including subsidies and support for their children's education (Wei, 2021). Some politicians and scholars even proposed revoking the population control policy completely. For example, a deputy to the National People's Congress, Chen Xiangqun, proposed fully lifting the family planning policy, first in Northeast China (Global Times, 2021).

The new three-children-per-couple policy has virtually ended China's population control. Instead, it has encouraged people to have more kids. The Chinese government's concern about its population has also changed from worrying about its too rapid increase to its too slow increase, aging, and maldistribution of the two genders.

Three Dominant Leaders' Influence on China's Population Control Policies

Generally speaking, China's population control policies and their implementations have been influenced strongly by three dominant leaders in China. During the first three periods between 1949 and 1979, the most influential leader was Mao Zedong, the chairman of the Central Committee of the CCP. During the fourth period between 1980 and 2015, the most influential leader was Deng Xiaoping although he has never held the highest official leading position in China. Since 2016, President Xi Jinping has become most influential. Understanding the dominant roles of these three leaders would help us understand why and how population control policies have changed and been implemented in China over the past seven decades.

Mao was the founding father of the People's Republic of China, and he was the chairman of the Communist Party until his death in 1976. Having been mostly influenced by Marxism and traditional Chinese culture, which considered people as essential for the country. According to Mao, there are numerous things in the world, but people are the most precious ones. Mao's dialectical cognizance recognized the potential negative impact of the huge Chinese population while he mostly perceived it as a positive force in China's socioeconomic development. When scholars and politicians worried about not having sufficient food for the population, Mao believed that revolution plus production could solve the problem. Therefore, he supported family planning yet tried to utilize the huge population in China's socioeconomic development.

Since Mao never believed that China's population was a major problem and seldom placed population control high on his government agenda, China's population control policy only changed gradually, from prohibiting birth control in the early 1950s to effective population control during the 1970s. During the second half of the 1950s, the purpose of China's family planning was to enable women to work and improve their education. During the 1960s, China adopted a family planning policy that advocated "later marriage and later birth, longer intervals between births and fewer children" to slow population growth, but the policy was only tested in limited areas, such as in Wendeng county in Shandong Province and in Shanghai Municipality. During the 1970s when Mao wanted to control population growth, the "later marriage" policy was implemented effectively nationwide.

Having established great prestige during the revolutionary years, Mao's perspective on population actually determined China's population control policies between 1949 and 1979. When Mao decided to mobilize the Chinese population to accelerate socioeconomic development, government population control efforts were swept aside. When China's population reached 800 million in 1969 and Mao wanted to control population growth, population control policies became effective, which is why when Mao demanded population control in the early 1970s, China's "later marriage" policy was implemented throughout the nation. As a result, China's population kept growing during the 1950s and 1960s. During the 1970s, however, population growth fell substantially. For example, from 1971 to 1979, China's birth rate declined from 30.65 per thousand to 17.82 per thousand, and the natural increase rate dropped from 23.33 per thousand in 1971 to 11.61 per thousand in 1979 (see Table 2.1).

During the fourth period between 1980 and 2015, Deng's perspectives on population became dominant. In 1953, Deng began to support family planning, and later, he continued supporting population control policies. However, his ideas about population control remained in the shadow of Mao's perspective, and Deng had only a limited impact on the Chinese government's population control policy between 1949 and 1979. After Mao's death in 1976, Deng gradually came to lead China, and his ideas about population control dominated China's policies.

Deng's political ideology was highly utilitarian, and his focus was almost exclusively on economic development. He was strongly influenced by the Western perspectives on population, including influence from the United States. Under Deng's dominance, the government's strategy was to control population growth to promote economic development, more specifically, to limit total population within 1.2 billion and quadruple its GNP by the end of the 20th century. Accordingly, the government revised the constitution in 1978, and for the first time, the constitution stated that the country advocates and promotes family planning. In 1980, the government adopted the one-birth-per-couple policy. With a single-minded focus on economic development, the government employed the constitution, administrative means, and economic measures to enforce population control.

Although the government made adjustment in the mid-1980s and issued permits to rural families to have a second child, the One-Birth-Per-Couple Policy was in effect until 2015. After 1992, the government employed more economic means to enforce the policy. Along with the rapid socioeconomic development, rapid urbanization, and considerably improved education, China's population growth rate plummeted from 11.87 per thousand in 1980 to 4.96 per thousand in 2015. At the same time, China's birth rate shrank from 18.21 per thousand in 1980 to 12.07 in 2015 (see Table 2.1).

Since 2016, China's population control policy was mostly influenced by Xi Jinping, who became the president of China and CCP chairman in 2013. Xi considers China's huge population as a fundamental, long-term, and strategic issue. He believes that China will continue to face the pressures of overpopulation for a long time, and the contradiction between population and development and between population and available resources will continue in China. Therefore, the government will continue its population control policy in the future (Wu and Hu, 2016). However, he also sees the positive effect of a large population and the negative side of the restrictive population control. For example, when giving a speech before the Indonesian parliament on October 3, 2013, Xi stated that the combined population of China and Indonesia was 1.6 billion people, and they could make a new miracle in history if they work together. At the same time, he also recognizes that China's aging population poses a new challenge to China's balanced population growth and security.

Under Xi's leadership, the Chinese government adopted a policy in 2016 that allowed any married couple to have two children. However, the new policy has not brought the expected increase in the birth rate in China, to say nothing of a rebound in births as many established demographers had worried. Then, in 2021, after the 2020 National Population Census clearly indicated that the Two-Children-Per-Couple Policy was not working, the government adopted another policy that allowed any married couple to have three children. If the number of married couples continues to drop as it did between 2013 and 2016 and the number of newborn babies does not increase considerably, the Chinese government will have to take greater steps to revise its population control policy in the future, including revoking the existing population control policy completely and allowing married couples to have as many children as they like.

It seems that during the period when Mao was dominant, the Chinese government perceived more positive effects from the Chinese population and attached a great value to people. Human beings were seen as producers as well as consumers. During the period dominated by Deng, the government focused on the negative effects of population growth and gave priority exclusively to economic development. Human beings were mostly seen as consumers or burdens on the nation. Therefore, under Mao's leadership, even when China had a planned economy, the government mostly did not require the Chinese population to grow according to the government plan. When Deng led the country, the government required the population to grow according to its plan and market mechanisms that were being introduced to spur economic development. Therefore, China's population control policy during the period dominated by Mao was encouraged and implemented through persuasion, but it was legally required and imperatively enforced during the period dominated by Deng. After Xi became the president of China, the government embarked on a more balanced strategy and paid attention to the negative aspects of the restrictive population control policies. Since 2013, population control policies have become more flexible and adjustments have been made more according to population realities.

Summary and Discussions

China's population control policies developed over five periods, starting with the founding of the PRC in 1949. The policies have been changed from limiting the use of contraceptives and abortion to promoting family planning between the 1950s and the 1970s. The "later marriage and birth, longer interval between births, and fewer children" policy of the 1970s slowed down China's population growth. Voluntary family planning programs became mandatory policy between 1980 and 2015, at which time China adopted and implemented its unique and controversial one-birth-per-couple policy, which further reduced China's birth rate below the replacement level. In 2016, the Chinese government adopted a Two-Children-Per-Couple Policy, and in 2021, the government adopted a Three-Children-Per-Couple Policy, easing population control when the nation faces an increasingly severe aging and unbalanced gender structures. Dramatic changes in the birth rate and natural increase rate show that China's population control policies have been effective in reducing China's population growth. The 2016 policy change has proved ineffective in increasing birth rates, though.

China's effective population control has been achieved mostly during two periods: One is between 1971 and 1979 when the Chinese government adopted and implemented the "later marriage and birth, longer interval between births, and fewer children" policy. As a result, China's per thousand birth rate was reduced by 42% from 30.65 in 1971 to 17.82 in 1979. The other period is between 1980 and 2015 when the government adopted and implemented the one-birth-per-couple policy. As a result, China's birth rate further reduced by 6.14 per thousand, from 18.21 in 1980 to 12.07 in 2015. During the 35 years between 1980 and 2015, China's per thousand birth rate was reduced by 34%. In comparison, the 12.83 per thousand birth rate reduction during the eight years between 1971 and 1979 was much greater than the 6.14 per thousand birth rate reduction during the 35 years between 1980 and 2015. Similarly, the reduction of 11.72 per thousand natural increase rate within eight years from 23.33 in 1971 to 11.61 in 1979 is much larger than the reduction of the 6.91 per thousand natural increase rate within 35 years from 11.87 in 1980 to 4.96 in 2015. In other words, the later marriage policy was much more effective than the one-birth-per-couple policy in terms of reducing the birth rate and the natural increase rate in China (see Figure 2.1).

Considering the substantial increase in per capita income, the improvement of woman's education and employment, and the rapid urbanization between 1980 and 2015, the one-birth-per-couple policy seems even less effective than the later marriage policy. However, when comparing the effectiveness of China's population control policies before 1980 and after 1980, we should consider that the reduction of the birth rate and the natural increase rate between 1980 and 2015 was based on the earlier reduction between 1971 and 1979, which could mean that the decline after 1980 was more difficult to achieve than during the earlier period. The fall in the birth and natural increase rates that occurred after 1980 was based on reductions that preceded 1980.

When compared with India, China's reduced population growth may have contributed substantially to its economic development. For example, China's per capita

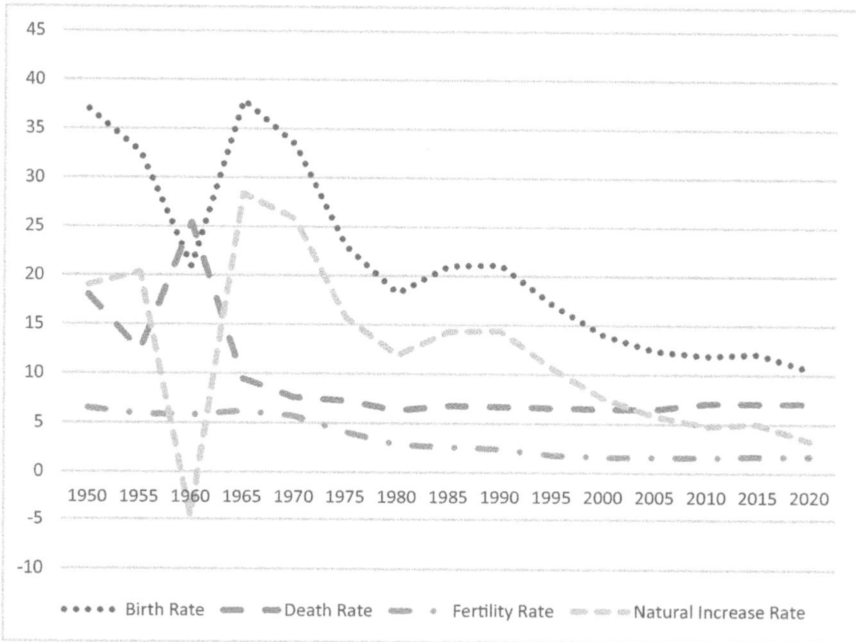

Figure 2.1 Birth Rate, Death Rate, Total Fertility, and Natural Increase Rate of China's Population

Sources:

1. National Bureau of Statistics of China. 2021. National Data, Population. Retrieved on September 21, 2022, at http://www.stats.gov.cn/tjsj/ndsj/2021/indexch.htm.
2. Total fertility rate was according to the Macrotrends (2021) data retrieved on April 7, 2021, from https://www.macrotrends.net/countries/CHN/china/populationAccording to a cross-country analysis by World Bank researchers, family planning programs independently accounted for a 40% fertility decline between 1965 and 1975 in an average developing country while socioeconomic change accounted for 27% of the observed decline (World Bank, 1984). Based on the World Bank research, it is reasonable to assume that China's later marriage policy and one-birth-per-couple policy have substantially reduced China's population growth even when the impact of socioeconomic development has been taken into consideration.

gross domestic product (GDP) increased considerably from about $113 in 1970 to about $4,550 in 2010. India's per capita GDP increased from about $112 to about $1,358 during the same period (World Bank, 2020). By 2022, China's per capita GDP increased to about $12,970 while India's per capita GDP increased to about $2,470 at 2022 prices (IMF, 2023). The difference in per capita GDP between China and India may, at least, partially be attributed to the difference in their population control policies and their implementations, or their different population growth.

However, the cost of the one-birth-per-couple policy was also obvious and long-lasting. Politically, the policy caused strong dissatisfaction among families that wanted more than one child. When an only child dies prematurely, many families suffer emotionally or financially for the rest of their lives. When abortions are carried out by coercion, they hurt not only women but also their families (China Development Research Foundation, 2012). The policy has also been severely criticized by Western political figures, religious groups, and human rights groups around the world.

Culturally, the single-child family structure has undermined traditional family values, which have always been essential to Chinese society. Family has always been at the center of Chinese life. It is the family and family relationships that are derived from and maintained by China's unique traditional values. When single children grow up without siblings, the number of their relatives is reduced, and their family value has been reduced, too. The single child is also affected in terms of its healthy maturation. According to Gross (2014), those who were born under the one-birth-per-couple policy after 1979 are less altruistic, less trustworthy, more risk-averse, and less competitive than those who were born before the policy was adopted. These influences will have a lasting impact on the Chinese society.

Population control policies have accelerated the demographic transition in Chinese society. While the population transition from high birth and death rates to a period of low birth and death rates took about 110 years in England, it took only three decades in China. At the same time, it also sped up the aging of China's population. Between 1982 and 2015, old age (65 or older) dependency increased from 8% to 14.3% of the population while childhood dependency (0–14) decreased from 54.6% to 22.6%. The total percentage of the dependent population (younger than 15 and older than 64) decreased from 62.8% in 1982 to 37.0% in 2015 (National Bureau of Statistics of China, 2020). On average, China's population was about ten years older than that of India in 2018. China's aging population may reduce its labor force and increase the cost of supporting the aged.

Sex imbalance is another problem mostly caused by the one-birth-per-couple policy. For example, the sex ratio among 5- to 9-year-old children was 118.55 males to 100 females in 2017. However, the sex ratio among the 30- to 34-year-old group who were born between 1983 and 1987 was 101.04 males to 100 females in 2017. It appears that the sex ratio increasingly skews toward males as China's birth rate declines. When the whole population is taken into consideration, the sex ratio was slightly reduced from 107.56 males to 100 females in 1953 to 105.2 males to 100 females in 2010 (China Development Research Foundation, 2012). China's sex ratio further reduced to 104.81 males to 100 females in 2017 (National Bureau of Statistics of China, 2018). This change may indicate that widely assumed gender imbalances may not be as bad as many assumed. The changes accelerated by the one-birth-per-couple policy may create new challenges to Chinese society but may not impact its socioeconomic development much more dramatically than in developed nations.

Therefore, if the Chinese government had continued its later marriage policy between 1980 and 2015, its population growth could have been sufficiently reduced along while it was undergoing rapid socioeconomic development. Since the policy implemented during the 1970s was much more socially acceptable and almost as effective as the one-birth-per-couple policy, political, social, familial, and demographic costs could have been smaller. The later birth policy would have been less criticized around the world, Chinese dissatisfaction would have been less pronounced, family and demographic structures could have been more appropriate, and the aging problem would most likely have been smaller.

The implementation of the two-children-per-couple policy indicates that population trends once set by social policy and socioeconomic development cannot be reversed easily. This phenomenon is similar to the problem that developed nations have faced in trying to increase their low birth rates. If the government had adopted the two-children-per-couple policy 20 years earlier, it might be more effective in altering China's population growth trend, thereby improving China's population structure. Better still, if China had continued its later marriage policy after 1980, its population structure and growth would have been more appropriate for long-term socioeconomic development. China's three-children-per-couple policy adopted in 2021, like the two-children-per-couple policy adopted in 2016, may not alter China's population growth rate or reduce the aging problem as much as expected. Chinese society has already developed into a stage that is not conducive to either marriage or population growth. To reverse current population growth trends and avoid future negative population growth, there needs to be a change in its population control policy today.

Note

1 Part of this chapter that has been revised and updated in this chapter was published in a chapter in the book, *China's Population: Problems, Thoughts and Policies* by Ashgate in 1999.

References

Bai, Jianfeng. 2014. "Elucidating Policy Permitting Couples to Have a Second Birth If One Spouse Is an Only Child". *People.cn.Beijing*. Retrieved on August, 22, 2014 from http://ft.people.com.cn/fangtanDetail.do?pid-141.

China Daily. 1991. "Birth Control Tops Priority". *China Daily*, June 19, p. 1.

China Development Research Foundation. 2012. *Development Report of China 2011/12, Population Change and Adjustment of Population Policy*. Beijing: China Development Press.

Deng, X. P. 1983. "Stick on the Four Principles", in *The Selected Works of Deng Xiaoping (1975–1982)*. Beijing: People's Press, 144–170.

Encyclopedia. 2020. "Population Policy in China". *Encyclopedia.com*. Retrieved on February 19, 2020 from www.encyclopedia.com/science/encyclopedias-almanacs-transcripts-and-maps/population-policy-china.

Global Times. 2021. "NE China Can Pilot Full Relaxation of Family Planning Policy to Ease Regional Population Decline: National Health Authority". *People's Daily*. February 19, 2021. Retrieved on September 9, 2022 frompdnews.cn.

Gross, Michael. 2014. "Where Next for China's Population Policy?" *Current Biology* 24(3): 97–100.

He, Yafu. 2013. *The Incontrollable Population Control: A Rethinking of China's Population Control Policies*. Beijing: China Development Press.

Hua, K. F. 1978. "Unite and Strive to Build a Modern and Powerful Socialist Country". *Peking Review*10.

IMF, 2023. "GDP Per Capita, Current Prices, U.S. Dollar Per Capita". *Map*. Retrieved on March 18, 2023 from https://www.imf.org/external/datamapper/NGDPDPC@WEO/OEMDC/ADVEC/WEOWORLD.

Jiang, Z. H. and L. G. Zhang. 1997. *A Report on China's Population*. Liaoning: Liaoning People's Press.

Liu, Yanqing. 2013a. "Experts Appeal for a Reform of Population Policy". *Chinese Economic Weekly* 10 (43): 40–42.

Liu, Z. 1984. *The Problems of Population Theory*. Beijing: Social Science Press of China.

Liu, Zhongliang. 2013b. *The Dangerous Future of a Huge Country: The Rise and Fall of Nations and Rethinking of China's Population Policy*. Beijing: Economic Science Publisher.

Macrotrends. 2021. "China Population 1950–2023". Retrieved on April 7, 2021 from www.macrotrends.net/countries/CHN/china/population.

National Bureau of Statistics of China. 2018. *China Statistical Yearbook, 2017*. Beijing: China Statistical Publishing House.

National Bureau of Statistics of China. 2020. *China Statistical Yearbook*. Beijing: China Statistical Publishing House.

National Bureau of Statistics of China. 2021. "National Data, Population". Retrieved on September 21, 2022 from www.stats.gov.cn/tjsj/ndsj/2021/indexch.htm.

Sanderson, W. C. and J. P. Tan. 1995. *Population in Asia*. Washington, DC: The World Bank

Stachel, Gregory. 2023. "Number of Births in China Falls to Record Low in 2021". *Learning English*. Retrieved on March 18, 2023 from https://learningenglish.voanews.com/a/number-of-births-in-china-falls-to-record-low-in-2021/6403546.html.

Tian, Xueyuan. 2009. *Sixty Years of China's Population Policy*. Beijing: Chinese Social Sciences Academy Press.

United Nations Department of Economic and Social Affairs/Population Division. 2022. "World Population Prospects 2022, Summary of Results". Retrieved on September 5, 2022 from www.un.org/development/desa/pd/sites/www.un.org.development.desa.pd/files/wpp2022_summary_of_results.pdf.

Wang, Gabe. 2018. "Population Change and the Social Factors That Affected the Changes in China and India". *Jiang Su Social Sciences* 2018 (5): 82–91.

Wei, Xueming. 2021. "Hopefully, New Family Planning Policy Will Lead to Healthy Population Growth". *China Daily*, October 19. Retrieved on September 9, 2022 frompdnews.cn.

World Bank. 1984. "World Development Report 1984". Retrieved on April 23, 2020 from https://openknowledge.worldbank.org/bitstream/handle/10986/5967/WDR%201984.

World Bank. 2020. "GDP Per Capita (Current US$)-China, India. World Bank National Accounts Data, and OECD National Accounts Data Files". Retrieved on April 19, 2020 from https://data.worldbank.org/indicator/NY.GDP.PCAP.CD?locations=CN-IN&most_recent_year_desc=false.

Wu, Jing and Hao Hu. 2016. "Xi Jing Ping's Important Instruction on Population and Family Planning". *Xing Hua Website*, May 18. Retrieved on January 12, 2017 fromhttp://news.xinhuanet.com/politics/2016-05/18/c_1118890622.htm.

Xinhua. 2021. "Xinhua Headlines: China Unveils Details of Three-Child Policy, Support Measures". *Xinhuanet*, July 20. Retrieved from www.xinhuanet.com/english/2021-07/21/c_1310073319.htm.

Xin Hua News Website. 2016. "The Decision of the Central Committee of the Chinese Communist Party and the State Council of China on the Implementation of the Two-child

Policy Nationwide and on the Reformation and Improvement of the Management and Services of Family Planning". Retrieved on April 17, 2020 from www.xinhuanet.com//politics/2016-01/05/c_1117678260.htm.

Yao, X. W. and H. Yin. 1994. *Basic Data of China's Population*. Beijing: Population Press of China.

Yi, Fuxian. 2012. *Big Country With an Empty Nest*. Beijing: China Development Press.

Zheng, Zhenzhen. 2013. "The Choice of Having a Second Child and Its Implication for Future Family Structure in China", in Buchanan, A. and Rotkirch, A. (eds) *Fertility Rates and Population Decline. Palgrave Macmillan Studies in Family and Intimate Life*. London: Palgrave Macmillan.

Zhou, P. 1986. "A Recall and Consideration of the Changes of Population Policy in the Early Period of the Republic". *Population Research* 1(6): 1–5.

3 Population Control Policies and Their Implementations in India[1]

Introduction

In 1952, India was the first major nation to adopt policies to control the growth of its enormous population. Despite seven decades of implementation, India's population has grown much more rapidly than the rest of the world. According to the estimations by the United Nations Department of Economic and Social Affairs/ Population Division (2022), India accounted for 14.9% of the world's population in 1950. That percentage climbed to 17.9% in 2020. By 2023, its population will overtake China's and become the world's most populous country.

What are India's population control policies, and how have they been implemented? With one of the most dynamic economies in the world and about 18% of the world's population, India's importance and its impact on the world will be increasingly significant. Therefore, this chapter describes Indian population control policies, how they have developed and changed, and how they have been implemented since the early 1950s.

Having played the most significant roles in India's struggle for independence, Mahatma Gandhi and Jawaharlal Nehru possessed unique and fundamental influence on Indians' perspectives on population and the policies that the nation adopted immediately after Independence. Therefore, this chapter will discuss their perspectives and influences on population control policies in India first.

Influences of Gandhi and Nehru

Even before Independence in 1947, leaders of India's anti-colonial movement expressed concern about the huge population and its potential impact on future development. Gandhi, the primary leader of India's independence movement, and Nehru, a leader of the nationalist movement and the first prime minister of India, had a fundamental influence on India's population control policies after Independence.

Although Gandhi was educated in England, he was not influenced by prevailing Western perspectives on population, which assumed that a huge population would affect socioeconomic development adversely and must be controlled for economic development. Gandhi's perspective on population was philosophical and based on concepts of social affection, the doctrine of non-possession, and trusteeship (Ranjan, 1999).

DOI: 10.4324/9781003307419-3

Gandhi did not believe India's population would be a problem. He once pointed out that with a proper land system and better agriculture and supplementary industry India was capable of supporting twice its population. He believed that growth was not and ought not to be regarded as a calamity to be avoided (a perspective similar to Mao's in the early 1950s in China). He also stated that contraceptives were an insult to womanhood (Mahatma Gandhi Media and Research Service, 2019). When people worried that overpopulation might hinder economic development, Gandhi countered that once a new social order was created and the society developed on its own terms, it would adjust itself and find its own solution to population growth problems. Therefore, Gandhi thought it unnecessary to have one or two isolated and narrowly defined interventions (Ranjan, 1999). When debating pioneering American feminist and early birth control activist Margaret Sanger in the 1930s, Gandhi spoke out against contraception.

Although Gandhi died before the government adopted and implemented any specific policy for population control, his perspective on population influenced ideas on population control in India. Two of his disciples, Rajkumari Amrit Kaur and Sushila Nayar, who took turns leading the Ministry of Health, waged a rearguard action against birth control during the 1950s and 1960s. When other government officials promoted birth control in the early 1950s, Kaur continued to insist that only the rhythm method was acceptable (Connelly, 2006).

Nehru had a perspective that was fundamentally influenced by prevailing Western perceptions on population. After observing the Industrial Revolution and the spread of modern technology that promoted the population growth in Europe, Nehru assumed that an eastward sweep of modern technology would result in a substantial population increase in India. Accordingly, he perceived India's population as a burden and weakness that needed to be productively organized (Nehru, 2004). On the other hand, he was also influenced by Communist ideology, preferring a socialistic way of development, and he was willing to adopt programs to control population growth. When he became premier, his ideas were fundamental to the adoption of population control policies in 1952 (Ranjan, 1999).

In fact, leading politicians like Nehru set out to address the population growth issue as early as in the 1940s. After the National Planning Committee was established in 1938 by Congress President and Indian National Army supreme leader Netaji Subhash Chandra Bose, a sub-committee was set up on population. Under the chairmanship of Nehru, the sub-committee recommended a gradual increase in marriage age; teaching contraception in medical colleges; special training for doctors, nurses, and health visitors; establishment of birth control clinics; provision of free contraceptives supply; local manufacture of contraceptives; a vigorous mass publicity campaign; education about population problems; and the introduction of a eugenic program for sterilization of persons suffering from genetic diseases (Aspalter, 2002). These ideas strongly influenced the adoption and the implementation of the population control policies by the Indian government after its independence in 1947. Gandhi's perspectives, however, continued to influence ordinary people in India and affected the implementation of the family planning programs.

Three Periods of Population Control Policies and Implementations

The development of population control policies and their implementations in India since the early 1950s can be roughly divided into three periods. The first, a service-providing policy period, took place between 1952 and 1961. The second was an imperative and target-oriented period between 1962 and 1977. The third, a voluntary period, has been ongoing since April 1977. Since population control policies have always been part of its 5-year plans for the socioeconomic development, I will follow the time frame of the government's 5-year plans.

1. Service-Providing Policy Period Between 1952 and 1961

During the first 9 years of population control, the government policy started in a modest way, and its efforts focused on providing services. In 1952, during the First Five-Year Plan period between 1951 and 1956, the Indian government assumed that rapid population growth would hinder socioeconomic development. Accordingly, it adopted a "family limitation and population control" program intended to assess the factors that contribute to rapid population growth, identify suitable techniques for family planning, devise methods to disseminate the knowledge and techniques for birth control, and provide advice on family planning (Ranjan, 1999). The goal of the program, backed by a 6.5 million rupees allocation, was vaguely defined as a program to reduce the birth rate to the extent necessary to stabilize the population at a level consistent with the requirements of the national economy (Planning Commission, 1952).

To implement the policy, the government used a natural and a clinical approach. The natural approach, also known as the Gandhian approach, followed Gandhi's belief that artificial birth control was impractical and would be misused. The Gandhian approach suggested abstinence and the rhythm method were the most suitable methods for Indians. There is little evidence to indicate that this approach ever worked to control India's population.

The clinical approach made hospitals and health care facilities provide birth control information to meet parent needs. It emphasized providing contraceptive services to couples. Although hospitals and health care facilities made birth control information available, the government did not aggressively encourage parents to use contraceptives to reduce their family size. As a result, the "family limitation and population control" program had little impact on population growth, and only 22% of the 6.5 million rupees fund was spent (Chaudhry, 1989).

During the Second Five-Year Plan, between 1956 and 1961, the federal government continued to implement its family limitation and population control program. State Family Planning Offices were established, and posts with officers were created in the states. Facilities for voluntary sterilization were also created. The Indian government substantially increased its funding for the population control programs to 49.7 million rupees. The distribution of contraceptives was extended through primary health centers.

Gradually, the clinic approach gained momentum and more services were made available at all hospitals and dispensaries throughout the country. The number of clinics was substantially increased from 147 to 4,165, and a sterilization operation was included in the family planning program. The distribution of contraceptives was extended through primary health centers and government-run hospitals, dispensaries, and maternity homes (Aspalter, 2002). At the same time, demographic research centers were established in Bombay, Calcutta, Delhi, and Trivandrum. In both rural and urban areas, contraceptives were issued either for free or at reduced prices to low-income families (Srinivasan, 2017).

However, while there was a supply of clinics, contraceptives, or even sterilizations for family planning, there was no demand for them. Both the Gandhi and clinical approaches remained ineffective because most people did think family planning unnecessary. With men dominating at home, women who were targeted by the program were virtually unable to make decisions on family planning (Ranjan, 1999). Although the government increased funding for population control programs, only 44% of the program's 49.7 million rupees budget was spent by the end of the Second Five-Year Plan (Chaudhry, 1989). The 1961 population census clearly indicated that Indian population growth was little affected; it kept growing rapidly.

After 9 years of population control policy, India's total fertility rate (TFR) reduced slightly from 5.91 children per woman in 1950 to 5.89 in 1961. The birth rate slightly reduced from 44.2 births per thousand in 1950 to 41.8 in 1961. While the death rate fell from 28.2 per thousand in 1950 to 21.9 in 1961, India's natural increase rate actually increased from 16.1 per thousand in 1951 to 20.2 in 1961. The total population increased from about 376 million in 1950 to about 460 million in 1961 (see Table 3.1). Population control policies during this period seem to have had little impact on population growth in India.

2. Imperative and Target-Oriented Policy Period Between 1962 and 1977

From 1962 to March 1977, Indian population controls changed gradually from service-providing programs to imperative and target-oriented population control policies that increased in intensity. During the Third Five-Year Plan, between 1961 and 1966, the government saw India's high birth rate as its greatest obstacle to economic development. In response, the government created a separate Department of Family Planning in the Ministry of Health and Family Planning, and it set a goal of reducing the birth rate to 25 per thousand by 1972. The demographic goals were specified state by state and district by district for each family planning program. The government also set fixed targets that family planning workers should meet for the number of people using contraceptives (Sidhu, 2016).

In order to stabilize population growth, the government increased funding for the family planning program to 270 million rupees and decided to increase the number of clinics fivefold. At the same time, every village and every town were directed to form a family planning committee, and "natural group leaders" were paid an "honorarium" of Rs. 4,000 to develop a "small family norm among their group" (Connelly, 2006).

In implementing the policies, the ineffective Gandhian and clinic approaches were replaced by an extension approach that stressed the role of intensive education among the masses. The plan was to be carried out by an army of extension educators. The government also provided facilities and advice to rural and urban communities. During the plan holiday period (a contingent plan when the original 5-year plan cannot be implemented or the gap between two 5-year plans) between 1967 and 1969, the family planning program was integrated with the public health program. The delivery of family planning services was extended through the commercial distribution of condoms. With generous international support, the government introduced a new system of incentive payments to those who availed of family planning practices. Monetary rewards were paid to family planning workers and officials who procured cases for sterilization. As a result of increased government efforts, nearly 92% of the allocated 270 million rupees fund was spent. The number of those using family planning services increased to more than two million (Chaudhry, 1989).

Table 3.1 India's Total Population, Total Fertility, Birth Rate, Death Rate, Natural Increase Rate, and Urbanization Percentage (1950–2020)

Year	*Population (Thousands)*	*Total Fertility*	*Birth Rate (per 1,000)*	*Death Rate (Per 1,000)*	*Natural Increase Rate (per 1,000)*	*Urbanization Percentage*
1950	376,325	5.91	44.20	28.20		
1951	382,377	5.91	44.00	27.60	16.1	
1952	388,799	5.90	43.80	27.00	16.8	
1953	395,544	5.90	43.60	26.40	17.3	
1954	402,579	5.90	43.40	25.90	17.8	
1955	409,881	5.90	43.20	25.30	18.1	
1956	417,443	5.90	42.90	24.70	18.4	
1957	425,271	5.90	42.70	24.10	18.8	
1958	433,381	5.90	42.50	23.60	19.1	
1959	441,799	5.90	42.30	23.00	19.4	
1960	450,548	5.89	42.10	22.50	19.8	17.9
1961	459,642	5.89	41.80	21.90	20.2	18.0
1962	469,077	5.89	41.60	21.40	20.5	18.2
1963	478,826	5.89	41.40	20.90	20.8	18.4
1964	488,848	5.86	41.10	20.40	20.9	18.6
1965	499,123	5.82	40.70	19.90	21.0	18.7
1966	509,632	5.86	40.40	19.40	21.1	18.9
1967	520,401	5.76	40.10	18.90	21.1	19.1
1968	531,514	5.72	39.80	18.40	21.4	19.3
1969	543,084	5.66	39.50	17.90	21.8	19.5
1970	555,190	5.60	39.20	17.50	22.3	19.7
1971	567,868	5.54	39.00	17.00	22.8	19.9
1972	581,087	5.47	38.70	16.50	23.3	20.3
1973	594,770	5.41	38.40	16.10	23.5	20.7
1974	608,803	5.32	38.10	15.70	23.6	21.0
1975	623,103	5.24	37.70	15.30	23.5	21.3
1976	637,630	5.15	37.40	14.90	23.3	21.7

Year	*Population (Thousands)*	*Total Fertility*	*Birth Rate (per 1,000)*	*Death Rate (Per 1,000)*	*Natural Increase Rate (per 1,000)*	*Urbanization Percentage*
1977	652,409	5.06	37.00	14.50	23.2	22.0
1978	667,500	4.97	36.70	14.00	23.1	22.4
1979	682,995	4.92	36.40	13.80	23.2	22.7
1980	698,653	4.86	36.20	13.50	23.4	23.1
1981	715,385	4.80	36.00	13.20	23.5	23.4
1982	732,239	4.74	35.80	13.00	23.6	23.7
1983	749,429	4.68	35.60	12.70	23.5	23.9
1984	766,833	4.60	35.00	12.50	23.2	24.1
1985	784,360	4.52	34.50	12.30	22.9	24.4
1986	801,975	4.43	34.00	12.00	22.5	24.6
1987	819,682	4.35	33.50	11.80	22.1	24.8
1988	837,469	4.27	33.00	11.60	21.7	25.1
1989	855,335	4.18	32.40	11.30	21.3	25.3
1990	873,278	4.09	31.80	11.00	21.0	25.6
1991	891,273	4.01	31.20	10.70	20.6	25.8
1992	909,307	3.92	30.60	10.50	20.2	26.0
1993	927,404	3.83	30.00	10.20	19.9	26.2
1994	945,602	3.76	29.50	10.00	19.6	26.4
1995	963,923	3.69	29.00	9.70	19.4	26.6
1996	982,365	3.62	28.60	9.50	19.1	26.8
1997	1,000,900	3.55	28.10	9.30	18.9	27.0
1998	1,019,484	3.48	27.60	9.10	18.6	27.2
1999	1,038,058	3.41	27.10	9.00	18.2	27.5
2000	1,056,576	3.35	26.60	8.80	17.8	27.7
2001	1,075,500	3.28	26.20	8.70	17.4	27.9
2002	1,093,317	3.21	25.70	8.50	17.0	28.2
2003	1,111,523	3.14	25.20	8.40	16.7	28.6
2004	1,129,623	3.07	24.80	8.30	16.3	28.9
2005	1,147,610	3.00	24.30	8.20	15.9	29.2
2006	1,165,486	2.93	23.80	8.00	15.6	29.6
2007	1,183,209	2.87	23.30	7.90	15.2	29.9
2008	1,200,670	2.80	22.80	7.80	14.8	30.3
2009	1,217,726	2.72	22.20	7.70	14.2	30.6
2010	1,234,281	2.64	21.50	7.60	13.6	30.9
2011	1,250,288	2.56	20.90	7.50	13.0	31.3
2012	1,265,780	2.48	20.20	7.40	12.4	31.6
2013	1,280,842	2.40	19.60	7.30	11.9	32.0
2014	1,295,601	2.37	19.30	7.30	11.5	32.4
2015	1,310,152	2.33	18.90	7.30	11.2	32.8
2016	1,324,517	2.30	18.60	7.30	11.1	33.2
2017	1,338,677	2.27	18.30	7.20	10.7	33.6
2018	1,352,642	2.24	18.00	7.20	10.4	34.0
2019	1,366,418	2.22	17.80	7.30	10.2	34.5
2020	1,380,004	2.20	17.60	7.30	9.9	

Sources: Data are by the Macrotrends which compiled the data according to the information provided by the United Nations. The data are retrieved on April 1, 2021, from www.macrotrends.net/countries/IND/india/fertility-rate.

During the Fourth Five-Year Plan period, between 1969 and 1974, Indira Gandhi, the daughter of Nehru, came to power and the Indian government intensified its population control. The government further increased the funding for family planning program to 3.15 billion rupees (Aspalter, 2002) and set a target to reduce the national birth rate to 32 per thousand by 1974 and further to reduce it to 2.5% within ten to 12 years (Ranjan, 1999).

To enforce the new population control policy and reach the set target, a cafeteria approach was introduced to make all possible contraceptive methods available. The cafeteria approach included the use of condoms, diaphragms, jelly, creams, and foam tablets for newly married couples; the use of intrauterine contraceptive devices (IUDs) for couples with one or two children; and sterilization for couples who wanted no more children. In fact, sterilization became a major strategy of the family planning program. In 1971, the government enacted the Medical Termination of Pregnancy Act to allow for abortions performed by a medical practitioner within the first 3 months of pregnancy, except in the states of Jammu and Kashmir both of which are mostly Muslim (McBride, 2012).

When IUDs were first introduced in family planning programs in the 1960s, they proved effective. However, user reports of internal bleeding and rumors soon set the program back, and the number of Indians using IUDs started to decline. Then, during the early 1970s, mass vasectomy camps were organized in different parts of the country and incentives, such as cash, encouraged sterilization. A group approach was also used to encourage men to participate with the number of men receiving vasectomies increasing from 3.8 million in 1970 and 1971 to 5.9 million in 1972 and 1973 (Chaudhry, 1989).

At the beginning of the Fifth Five-Year Plan between 1974 and 1979, Indian policy makers strongly believed that excessive family size had to be integrated into a general development strategy (Heitzman and Worden, 1996). Therefore, a new target was set to reduce the birth rate to 30 per thousand by 1979 and to 25 per thousand by 1984. To reach the newly set goal, the Indian Parliament passed the National Population Policy in April 1976. The new 18-point policy aimed at making a frontal attack on the problems of population (Srinivasan, 2017).

Specifically, the new policy raised the minimum age of marriage from 15 to 18 years for females and from 18 to 21 years for males. It also increased monetary compensation for sterilization; on the basis of the 1971 census, it froze people's representation in the Lok Sabha and state legislatures through 2001; fixed the devolution of taxes, duties, and sanctions of grant-in-aid on the population figures of 1971, again through 2001; made 8% of the central government's assistance to state plans contingent on meeting performance benchmarks in family planning; and introduced compulsory sterilization and specific incentives and disincentives to use family planning (Ranjan, 1999). As for the compulsory sterilization, the federal government let state governments make rules and decisions (Chaudhry, 1989).

Along with the new policy, education about population problems became part of the school curriculum. In some areas, government-enforced sterilization was part of the measures for birth control. Female health workers and childhood nutrition workers received financial incentives from the Indian government to meet the yearly sterilization quotas, and health care workers who failed to meet their quotas risked losing their jobs. With the use of coercion, achievements were made in all Indian states, and some even exceeded their targets (Chaudhry, 1989). The emergency period imposed by Prime Minister Indira Gandhi between June 1975 and March 1977 allowed the government to exercise its power ruthlessly and enforce mass sterilization programs. When most of Gandhi's political opponents were imprisoned and the press was censored, Indira Gandhi's son, Sanjay Gandhi, spearheaded a forced mass-sterilization campaign.

> Vasectomies were performed in many government offices, schools, large railway stations, etc. The vasectomy booths set up in the Church gate and VT stations in Mumbai became notorious because of their ruthless nature: they gathered young male passengers getting off the electric trains and made them pass through the vasectomy booths where they were sterilized, unless they carried a card saying they have already been sterilized.
>
> (Srinivasan, 2017: 32–33)

As a result, India's population control became much more effective. Between 1976 and 1977, a total of 8.26 million sterilizations were performed, more than the total number done in the previous 4 years (Srinivasan, 2017). Yet, anger increased among the Indian people. During this period, the family planning program focused mainly on terminal methods and the program received pushback due to rigid implementation of a target-based approach (Department of Family Welfare, Ministry of Health and Family Welfare, Government of India, 1997). Coercive measures and government-enforced sterilizations angered the general population. As a result, Indira Gandhi's government, which adopted and enforced the policy, was voted out in the 1977 election. At the same time, the ruling Congress Party also lost elections in most of the states that it had formerly ruled (Kamal and Meyer, 1977). Consequently, the new government, dominated by the Janata Party, ruled out the use of coercion in family planning.

Although the Indian government sought to control population growth, the national birth rate was only reduced from 41.6 per thousand in 1962 to 37.0 per thousand in 1977. The TFR was also reduced from 5.89 in 1962 to 5.06 in 1977 while the death rate reduced from 21.4 per thousand in 1962 to 14.5 per thousand in 1977. However, the national natural increase rate increased from 20.5 per thousand in 1962 to 23.2 per thousand in 1977. The total population increased from about 469 million in 1962 to about 652 million in 1977 (see Table 3.1).

3. Voluntary Policy Period Since April 1977

Starting in April 1977, the Indian population control policy gradually changed from an imperative and target-oriented policy to a comprehensive social development plan, although some targets have been maintained. The coercive measures have mostly been replaced by voluntary efforts, and population control has become indirect. The new population control policy excluded the use of compulsory sterilizations. Nevertheless, the Indian government continued efforts to reduce the population. Sterilization has gradually shifted to women. In 1978, the minimum marriage age of 18 for girls and 21 for boys became law. Implementation remains weak, however, and marriages continue to take place for girls below the age of 18 (Srinivasan, 2017).

During the Sixth Five-Year Plan period between 1980 and 1985, the government relaxed its population control policy and changed the name of the program from family planning to "family welfare," explaining that maternal and child health services and nutrition should be part of any population control strategy. At the same time, population control became part of government policy to eradicate poverty and improve the Indian standard of living. The government also postponed the target (set by the Fifth Five-Year Plan) of reducing the birth rate to 30 per thousand in 1982 and 1983 instead of by 1979.

The Plan's long-term goals were to reduce the average family size from 4.2 children in 1979 to 2.3; reduce the birth rate from 33 per thousand in 1978 to 21 per thousand by 2001; reduce the death rate from 14 per thousand in 1978 to 9 per thousand; and halve the infant mortality rate from 129 to 60 or less by 2001. The short-term goals were to carry out 22 million sterilizations, have 22 million IUDs inserted, and increase the number of users of condoms, oral contraceptives, and other conventional methods to 11 million in the period from 1984 to 1985. During this period, the government's funding further increased to 10.87 billion rupees and the family planning programs further extended to rural areas through the network of primary health centers and sub-centers (Chaudhry, 1989). At the same time, efforts were also expended on promoting longer intervals between births, although few people actually paid attention to the policy.

The most fundamental change in Indian population control policy since April 1977 was that family planning became mostly voluntary. As a result of the political fallout of the 1977 election, the Indian government now put more emphasis on incentives to attract people to accept family planning instead of coercive measures. The federal government still gave priority to India's rapidly growing population. When the government set long-term policy goals rather than shorter ones, the targets for family planning were also substantially reduced. Unlike the early days of population control policy, which focused on reducing fertility rates through contraception, the government now extended its efforts to maternal and child health services. The cafeteria approach continued, for it recognized differences among the population and attempted to meet different people's needs (Ranjan, 1999; Aspalter, 2002). During the Sixth Five-Year Plan, the government allocated 10.78 billion rupees for family welfare programs, but the actual spending was estimated at 14.48 billion rupees. However, almost no targets in population control were reached (Srinivasan, 2017).

During the Seventh Five-Year Plan period between 1986 and 1991, population control policies extended to including specific and general goals, both long term and short term. The long-term goal was to fix the net reproduction rate to be achieved by 2001 and the short-term goal focused on female age at marriage and the practice of contraception. The specific goal was to promote a two-child norm through independent choice of family planning methods that were most suitable to users (Ranjan, 1999). The government efforts in population control further extended to increase the literacy rate of the population, especially of women; to improve the status of women by improving their employment opportunities; and to improve the health of mothers and children. The government also adopted communication strategies, such as multimedia and interpersonal communication to increase family planning awareness (Sidhu, 2016).

During this period, four special family planning projects were implemented. The first was the implementation of the All-India Hospitals Post-Partum Program at district- and sub-district-level hospitals. The second was the reorganization of primary health care facilities in urban slum areas. The third was the reservation of a specified number of hospital beds for tubal ligature operations. And the fourth was the renovation or remodeling of intrauterine contraceptive devices rooms in rural family welfare centers attached to primary health care facilities (Heitzman and Worden, 1996). In implementing the population control policies, the government also tried to make it a people's movement and decentralized planning and implementation of the programs. Despite these developments in promoting family planning, the 1991 census indicated that India continued to have one of the world's most rapidly growing populations.

For the Eighth Five-Year Plan period, between 1992 and 1997, population control remained a priority even as the government attempted to introduce target-free approaches and changed the national plans to localized area plans. In 1996, the Indian government announced a new national population control policy that eliminated numerical targets (Donaldson, 2002). The Indian government sought to control its population growth indirectly, not through specific targets. Government focus shifted toward human development, such as employment, education, and public health.

In implementing the new population control policy, the government adopted new indirect measures, shifting its emphasis from the couple protection rate to lowering the birth rate, giving large shares of central government assistance to the better performing states, involving non-government organizations and community leaders, improving women's status through poverty alleviation and employment, improving training and infrastructure, reducing infant mortality and maternal mortality rates, and introducing population study in schools and colleges (Shah, 2019). However, targets remained in some states and were reinstated in others (Khan and Townsend, 1998). Health care workers who did not meet their quotas risked losing their jobs. Worse still, the set targets often encouraged health care workers to misinform women about the health impacts of sterilization (McBride, 2012).

During the Ninth Five-Year Plan period, between 1997 and 2002, the National Commission on Population initiated a plan, National Population Policy 2000 (NPP, 2000), which "provide[d] a policy framework for advancing goals and prioritizing strategies during the next decades, to meet the reproductive and child health needs of the people of India, and to achieve net replacement levels (TFR [total fertility rate]) by 2010" (Department of Family Welfare, Ministry of Health and Family Welfare, Government of India, 2002: 2).

This new policy addressed contraception, health care infrastructure, and reproductive health care. The program's immediate objective was to address unmet needs for contraception, health care infrastructure, and health personnel and to provide integrated service delivery for basic reproductive and intersectoral operational strategies. The medium objective was to lower the TFR to the replacement level by 2010. The long-term objective was to achieve a stable population by 2045, at a level consistent with the requirements of sustainable economic growth, social development, and environmental protection (Department of Family Welfare, Ministry of Health and Family Welfare, Government of India, 2002).

India's National Population Policy 2000 has decentralized decision making to local government and improved coordination between the government and the local and non-government organizations. The program requires more funding for the program, the improvement of health care infrastructure and services, and the empowerment of women (Anupama, 2015). The program that is uniformly applicable to the whole country includes giving more emphasis on spacing methods like IUDs; setting certain days available at all facilities; establishing quality assurance committees at state and district levels to provide quality care in family planning services; providing insurance for deaths, complications, and failures caused by sterilization; compensating those who accept sterilizations; and increasing male participation in family planning (Oliveboard, 2021).

During the Tenth Five-Year Plan period, between 2002 and 2007, Indian population control efforts continued to shift from demographic targets to enabling couples to achieve their reproductive goals, from method-specific contraceptive targets to unmet needs for contraception to reduce unwanted pregnancies, from family planning to health care for women and children, from centrally defined targets to community need assessment and decentralized area-specific micro-planning and implementation of programs, from quantitative coverage to quality and content of care, from women-centered programs to the health care needs of the family with emphasis on the involvement of men in planned parenthood, from supply-driven service delivery to need and demand-driven service, and from service provision based on providers' perception to addressing choices and the convenience of the receiving couples (Shah, 2019).

During the Eleventh Five-Year Plan, between 2007 and 2012, the government aimed to reduce the total fertility to 2.1 by 2012. To achieve this goal, the government planned to expand family choices of contraceptives, improve social marketing, increase male involvement, enhance the role of the mass media for behavioral change, and disseminate contraceptives through the satisfied users. Recently, the Indian government's population control policy extended more services, including delivering contraceptives to the doorsteps of beneficiaries, providing counseling for newly married couples to delay first birth for 2 years, and for couples with one child to put off a second child for 3 years.

Since the Indian government mostly changed its quota-oriented population control policy in 1978 and adopted new, mostly voluntary measures or approaches, the Indian population control policies and their implementations may have become more effective, for India's ten-year increase rate reduced from 21.5% for the period between 1991 and 2001 to 17% during the 2001–2011 period (United Nations Department of Economic and Social Affairs/Population Division, 2017). Nevertheless, some scholars and politicians remained highly concerned about overpopulation in India. In 2016, Prahalad Singh Patel, a legislator from the central Indian state of Madhya Pradesh, introduced a population control bill to Parliament. The bill limits each married couple to have not more than two children in light of rising poverty, a decline in jobs, and a poor literacy rate in India's booming population. The bill, however, has never come to a vote. Scholars, such as B. Paswan, the head of the Department of Population Policies and Programs at the International Institute for Population Sciences believed that the proposition was simply not realistic. The Indian government had no plans to implement such a policy, and no political parties would support the government's adoption of such a policy (Gupta, 2019).

Nevertheless, India's population control seems to have become much more effective since April 1977. Although India's total population increased from about 668 million in 1978 to about 1,393 million in 2021, the birth rate fell from 36.7 per thousand in 1978 to 17.4 per thousand in 2021. The TFR also declined from 4.97 in 1978 to 2.18 in 2021. Similarly, the natural increase rate was reduced from 23.1 per thousand in 1978 to 9.7 per thousand in 2021 (see Table 3.1).

Summary and Discussions

During the service-providing policy period between 1952 and 1961, most Indian population control policies called on the public to engage in family planning practices, and government efforts were focused on providing information and services to potential users of contraceptives. The goal of the policy was not specifically defined, and efforts were ineffective because little demand existed for the services and family planning information supplied by clinics and health institutions. Population control policies and their implementations seemed to have little impact on the population growth in India. From 1950 to 1960, India's ten-year population growth rate was 19.5%, which was about 1.1% higher than China's growth rate (United Nations Department of Economic and Social Affairs/Population Division, 2017). During the 1950s, China did not have population control and actually prohibited contraceptives and abortion before 1955 (Wang, 1999). In both 1950 and 1960, India's percentage of the world's total population remained at 14.9%, which means that India's population was growing as rapidly as that of the world (see Table 3.2).

During the imperative and target-oriented period between 1962 and March 1977, the Indian population control moved gradually from a service-providing program to an imperative and target-oriented policy. The government set specific targets and adopted coercive measures to reach the set targets. The policy implementation gradually changed from promotion of contraception to sterilization. The new policy and its implementation became more effective mostly in terms of enlisting family planning users and sterilizations than in the previous period. However, the achievements recorded on paper have not always translated into reduced population growth.

Table 3.2 Population Changes in India

Year	*Total Population*	*Ten-Year Increase*	*Percentage of World's Population*	*Total World Population*
1950	376,325,000		14.9%	2,525,149,000
1960	449,662,000	19.5%	14.9%	3,018,344,000
1970	553,943,000	23.2%	15.0%	3,682,488,000
1980	697,230,000	25.9%	15.7%	4,439,632,000
1990	870,602,000	24.9%	16.4%	5,309,668,000
2000	1,053,481,000	21.0%	17.2%	6,126,622,000
2010	1,230,985,000	16.8%	17.8%	6,929,725,000
2020	1,388,859,000	12.8%	17.9%	7,758,157,000

Source: United Nations Department of Economic and Social Affairs/Population Division (2017). World Population Prospects: The 2015 Revision, Volume I: Comprehensive Tables (Pages: 18–21). Retrieved on January 18, 2017 at: https://esa.un.org/unpd/wpp/Publications/Files/WPP2015_Volume-I_Comprehensive-Tables.pdf.

The new population control policies and the coercive measures used in implementing the policies were more than Indian society could accommodate. As a result, the social population control policy was badly defeated in the political arena, which set population control back in India in 1977. The coercive measures used in population control policy implementation seemed not only inappropriate for Indian society but also ineffective in terms of population control. Instead of reducing population growth more effectively, the ten-year population growth rate was substantially increased from a population increase of about 19.5% between 1950 and 1960 to about 25.9% between 1970 and 1980. India's percentage of the world's population climbed from about 14.9% in 1960 to about 15.7% in 1980, which means that the Indian population increased more rapidly than that of the world in this period even though the government used coercive measures to carry out sterilization and tightened its population control (see Table 3.2).

After April 1977, population control policies have become much less focused and the measures utilized to implement the policies have become mostly voluntary, as the Indian government proclaimed they would. Although the Indian government maintained the priority of population control in its national socioeconomic development plans, it adopted indirect policies and measures to control growth. This change integrated health care and social development with family planning services. At the same time, Indian population control policies have gradually changed from time-bound and target-oriented policies to mostly target-free policies, and the implementation measures have also changed from compulsory approaches to voluntary approaches.

Although population control policies since April 1977 have been unfocused, changing constantly, and seldom reached, this third period of population control policies and their implementations seem to have fit Indian social conditions and political structures much better. Decentralized policies seem more suitable than the centralized ones to India's federal structure. When different states or areas have different religions and degrees of socioeconomic development, they need different measures to control population growth.

Population control policies and their implementations since April 1977 have become more effective. Between 1980 and 2010, the ten-year population increase rate decreased from 25.9% between 1970 and 1980 to 16.8% between 2000 and 2010 (see Table 3.2). The annual natural increase rate also reduced from 23.1 per thousand in 1978 to 9.7 per thousand in 2021. Figure 3.1 clearly demonstrates the development trend in India (see Figure 3.1). Of course, reduction of the population increase rate in India may also result from accelerated socioeconomic development and other social changes since 1991.

However, the Indian population control policies and their implementations were not as effective as those of other countries. For example, India's percentage of the world's total population increased from about 15.7% in 1980 to about 17.9% in 2020, which means that the population growth rate in India was 2.2% greater than the average growth rate in the world between 1980 and 2020. At the same time, India's percentage of Asia's total population also increased from about 26.6% in 1980 to about 29.5% in 2010. In 2023, India's population will overtake China's and become the most populous country in the world (United Nations Department of Economic and Social Affairs/Population Division, 2022).

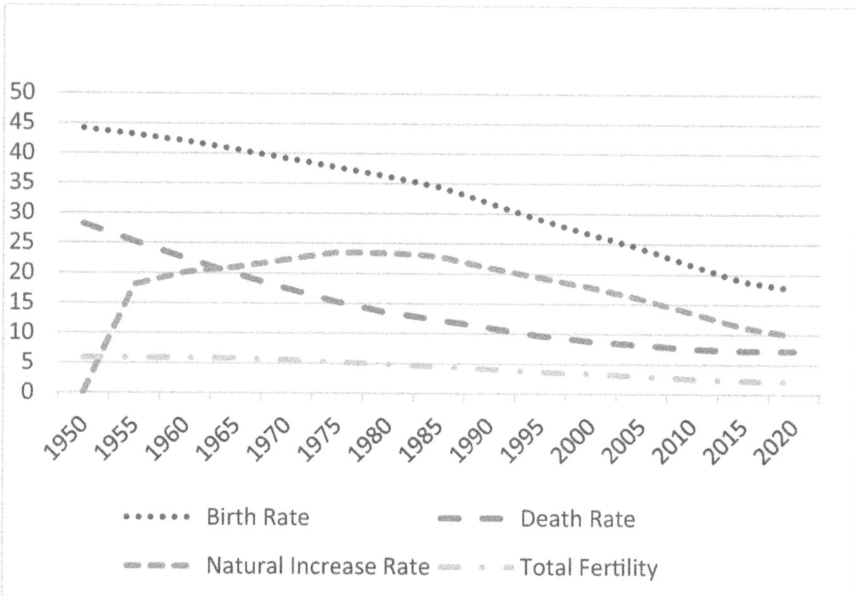

Figure 3.1 Birth Rate, Death Rate, Total Fertility, and Natural Increase Rate of India's Population

Sources: Data are by the Macrotrends which compiled the data according to the information provided by the United Nations. The data are retrieved on April 1, 2021, from https://www.macrotrends.net/countries/IND/india/fertility-rate.

India's enormous and rapidly increasing population may continue to put great pressure on socioeconomic development, natural resources, and the environment in India although the young population may allow India to have some demographic dividend. India's population change seems to indicate that a restrictive population control policy and coercive implementation of the policy may not work as well as many people have assumed. Between 1962 and 1977 when the Indian government adopted imperative and target-oriented policies and applied coercive measures to implement population control policies, the Indian population increased more rapidly than either the service-providing policy period between 1952 and 1961 or the voluntary period after April 1977.

China's population control experience may also support such an understanding. For example, between 1971 and 1980, the Chinese government began to call on unmarried people to marry and give birth later, increase the intervals between births, and have fewer children voluntarily. China's birth rate reduced from 30.7 per thousand in 1971 to 18.2 per thousand in 1980. Similarly, China's natural increase rate also reduced from 23.3 per thousand in 1971 to 11.9 per thousand in 1980. However, after China adopted the restrictive one-birth-per-couple policy and began to implement the policy coercively in 1980, the birth rate in China actually increased from 18.2 per thousand in 1980 to 21.1 per thousand in 1990. During the same period, China's natural increase rate also increased from 11.9 per thousand in 1980 to 14.4 per thousand in 1990 (Wang, 1999). The highly intense and coercive implementation of the one-birth-per-couple policy during the 1980s reduced birth and natural increase rates less than voluntary family planning had called for in the 1970s.

Although China's population growth has substantially reduced between the 1960s and 2010s, the rapid reduction of population growth should be attributed more to state-owned or collective economic structures that began in the later 1970s or to rapid socioeconomic development after the 1980s. Compared to India, substantial improvements in education and women's status in China also contributed to its population control (Wang, 2018).

India was the first major nation to adopt and implement policies to control the growth of its population; however, the policies were not often well defined, and they changed constantly. Policy implementation usually lacked focus and shifted periodically. Consequently, the Indian government's goals for population control were seldom reached and had to be revised repeatedly. This phenomenon was a reflection of the country's traditional and highly diversified social reality. For example, almost every person in India is religious, 66% of its population lives in rural areas, about 40% of women are illiterate (CIA, 2019), men and women are still not treated equally, and the caste system still affects society fundamentally.

Indian society is highly diversified. For example, India has not only the vast majority of the world's Hindus but also the world's second largest group of Muslims (Majumdar, 2018). Hinduism alone has 33 types of gods and goddesses (some Indians believe that there are 33 million). With diversified religions, there are high levels of religion-related social hostilities (Majumdar, 2018). Similar to the diversity of religions, there are 22 official languages and more than 19,569 mother tongues (Gulf News, 2019).

Socially, Indians were divided into five castes and the main castes were further divided into about 3,000 castes and 25,000 sub-castes. Although the caste system has been outlawed, it still affects the society fundamentally. Communal tensions between different castes have long plagued Indian society. This unique social reality may affect not only the population control policies and their implementations but also the functioning of society. Within such a traditional and highly diversified society, population control can be advocated or promoted, but cannot be forced or implemented effectively. To conclude, social conditions not only shape social policies but also determine the effectiveness of the policy implementations. Another fundamental factor that has affected India's population control is poverty. Much of India's population increase has occurred among the poorest population and in poorer states. The ineffectiveness of family planning programs can be primarily attributed to the problem of poverty (Gupta, 2002).

Therefore, a more effective measure to reduce population growth in this traditional and highly diversified society would be comprehensive socioeconomic development. Such development would include achieving equal status for women and lower-caste people and improving education, economic development, urbanization, and the modernization of society. When socioeconomic conditions improve, birth rates will fall and overpopulation problems will be reduced. Indira Gandhi would have agreed with this statement. After she returned to power in 1980 and was asked in a television interview, "Do you see any alternative for economic viability for the nation in the face of failure to curb population growth rate to a manageable proportion?" The real answer, she countered, of course, was development (Gandhi and Chhabra, 1981: 168). Bose (1981), a prominent social scientist associated with the Institute of Economic Growth of Delhi University, noted that family planning can succeed only when development planning succeeds.

Having studied population concerns in India, Krishnamurthy Srinivasan, an honorary professor at the Institute for Social and Economic Change at Bengaluru, seems quite disappointed at India's population control policies. He comments as follows:

> The fundamental issues in India's population remain almost essentially the same as they were at the time of independence in 1947: its large size, large number of unwanted births still occurring, easily avoidable deaths mostly among children, preventing very early marriages especially marriages in childhood, employment generation and eradication of poverty, ensuring that the various benefits aimed at the poor or those below the poverty line reach them and none else and improving gender equality. We had these concerns seven decades ago, and we still have them, though not with the same intensity and to the same extent but even now despite the wherewithal to handle them efficiently.
>
> (Srinivasan, 2017: 250)

Noting that other Asian countries or regions, such as China, Korea, Malaysia, Taiwan, and Thailand, all of which launched their developmental and population programs much later than did India, have done better, Srinivasan asks, "Where have we gone wrong" (2017: 250)? Professor Srinivasan has identified a few problems, such as wrong planning for development; continued prevalence of child marriages; allowing the slowing down of family planning efforts under the guise of integration of family planning programs with other programs; having uniform demographic goals for states at different stages of demographic transition; and the ineffectiveness of the organization and health systems in different states. He advises the Indian government to improve its population control policies and implementations.

Nevertheless, with multiple social factors hindering the implementation of population control policies in India and shortcomings in population control policies, the Indian society has slowly gone through the demographic transition from a high birth rate–high death rate to a low birth rate–low death rate. Within 70 years between 1951 and 2021, India's TFR has changed from 5.91 to 2.18, the birth rate has changed from 44.2 to 17.4 per thousand, and the death rate has also changed from 28.2 to 7.3 per thousand population. At the same time, India's natural increase rate has also reduced from 16.1 to 9.7 per thousand. This relatively slow transition may force Indian society to bear the burden of overpopulation for many more years, but it also allows society more leeway to adjust its socioeconomic development than those societies that have made a more rapid demographic transition.

Note

1 This chapter is a revised and expanded version of an article, "Population Control Policies and Implementations in India," published by the *Journal of Sociology and Social Work*, Vol. 7 (2): 135–144 in 2019.

References

Anupama, U. 2015. "National Population Policy 2000, AN EMMRC, Patiala Presentation". Retrieved on February 8, 2019 from www.youtube.com/watch?v=rZwOAgu304E.

Aspalter, C. 2002. "Population Policy in India". *The International Journal of Sociology and Social Policy* 22 (11–12): 48–72.

Bose, Ashish. 1981. "Commentary". *Population and Development Review* 7 (1): 170–171.

Central Intelligence Agency. 2019. "The World Factbook, India". Retrieved on March 22, 2019 from www.cia.gov/library/PUBLICATIONS/the-world-factbook/geos/in.html.

Chaudhry, M. D. 1989. "Population Policy in India". *Population and Environment: A Journal of Interdisciplinary Studies* 11(2): 101–121.

CIA. 2019. "'People and Society'. The World Factbook". Retrieved on March 19, 2023 from https://www.cia.gov/the-world-factbook/countries/india/#people-and-society

Connelly, M. 2006. "Population Control in India: Prologue to the Emergency Period". *Population and Development Review* 32(4): 629–667.

Department of Family Welfare, Ministry of Health and Family Welfare, Government of India. 1997. *Reproductive Health and Child Health Programme: Schemes for Implementation*. New Delhi: Ministry of Health and Family Welfare.

Department of Family Welfare, Ministry of Health and Family Welfare, Government of India. 2002. "Introduction", in *National Population Policy 2000 (Reprint 2002)*. New

Delhi: Nirman Bhawan. Retrieved on March 10, 2019 from https://mohfw.gov.in/sites/default/files/26953755641410949469%20%281%29.pdf.

Donaldson, P. J. 2002. "The Elimination of Contraceptive Acceptor Targets and the Evolution of Population Policy in India". *Population Studies* 56: 97–110.

Gandhi, I. and R. Chhabra. 1981. "Population Policy in India: Two Comments". *Population and Development Review* 7 (1): 168–171.

Gulf News, Asia. 2019. "Census: More Than 19,500 Languages Spoken in India as Mother Tongues". Retrieved on March 30, 2019 from https://gulfnews.com/world/asia/india/census-more-than-19500-languages-spoken-in-india-as-mother-tongues-1.2244791.

Gupta, A. 2002. *A Billion Is Enough: India's Population Problem – A Way Out*. Chandigarh: Unistar Books Pvt, Ltd.

Gupta, Swati. 2019. "A Two-child Policy in Overpopulated India? It Won't Work, Say Experts". *CNN*, January 21. Retrieved on May 9, 2020 from www.cnn.com/2019/01/21/health/india-two-child-policy-debate/index.html.

Heitzman, J. and R. L. Worden. 1996. *India, a Country Study. Federal Research Division, Library of Congress*. Washington, DC: U.S. Government Printing Office.

Kamal, K. L. and R. C. Meyer. 1977. *Democratic Politics in India*. New Delhi: Vikas Publishing.

Khan, M. E. and J. W. Townsend. 1998. "Has the Indian Family Welfare Program Lost Momentum Under the Target-Free Approach? Emerging Evidence". Paper Prepared for a World Bank Workshop on the Target-Free Approach. New Delhi, April 2–3.

Mahatma Gandhi Media and Research Service. 2019. "Thus Spake Gandhi, Select Quotations by Mahatma Gandhi, Birth Control". *Gandhiserve Foundation*. Retrieved on March 22, 2019 from www.gandhiservefoundation.org/about-mahatma-gandhi/thus-spake-gandhi/birth-control-1/.

Majumdar, S. 2018. "5 Facts about Religion in India". *Facttank: News in the Numbers. Pew Research Center*, June 29. Retrieved from www.pewresearch.org/fact-tank/2018/06/29/5-facts-about-religion-in-india/.

McBride, M. 2012. "History of Population Control in India". *Eye on Asia*. Retrieved on March 2, 2019 from https://humanrightsinasia.wordpress.com/2012/07/31/history-of-population-control-in-india/.

Nehru, J. 2004. *The Discovery of India*. East Rutherford, NJ: Penguin Books.

Oliveboard. 2021. "Evaluation of Population Control Policies in India-Relevance, Population Policy". Retrieved on March 18, 2023 from https://www.oliveboard.in/blog/evolution-of-population-control-policies-in-india/.

Planning Commission, Government of India. 1952. *First Five-Year Plan 1951–1956*. New Delhi: Government of Indian Press.

Ranjan, A. 1999. *Population and Development: The Indian Perspective*. Datia: Shyam Institute.

Shah, S. 2019. "Population Policy of India". *Sociology Discussion*. Retrieved on March 4, 2019 from www.sociologydiscussion.com/population/population-policy-population-policy-of-india/2377.

Sidhu, S. S. 2016. "Population Policy in India, Key Factors". *Online Lecture, YouTube*. Retrieved on February 7, 2019 from www.youtube.com/watch?v=d_F9x3Y-D94.

Srinivasan, K. 2017. *Population Concerns in India: Shifting Trends, Policies, and Programs*. New Delhi: Sage Publications India Pvt Ltd.

United Nations Department of Economic and Social Affairs/Population Division. 2017. *World Population Prospects: The 2015 Revision*. Vol I. Comprehensive Tables, pp. 18–21. Retrieved on January 18, 2017 from https://esa.un.org/unpd/wpp/Publications/Files/WPP2015_Volume-I_Comprehensive-Tables.pdf.

United Nations Department of Economic and Social Affairs/Population Division. 2022. "World Population Prospects 2022, Summary of Results". Retrieved on September 5, 2022 from www.un.org/development/desa/pd/sites/www.un.org.development.desa.pd/files/wpp2022_summary_of_results.pdf.

Wang, G. T. 1999. *China's Population: Problems, Thoughts and Policies*. Aldershot: Ashgate Publishing Limited.

Wang, G. T. 2018. "The Population Change and the Social Factors That Affected the Change in China and India". *Jiang Su Social Sciences* 2018 (5): 82–91.

4 A Comparison of Population Control Policies and Their Implementations in China and India

Introduction

Although China and India have adopted policies to control their enormous populations since the 1950s, they have grown and changed differently. In 1950, China's population was 544 million and India's population was 376 million (Wang, 2018). At that time, India's population was 69.2% of China's population. Seventy years later, in 2020, however, China's population is 1,403 million and India's population is 1,389 million (United Nations Department of Economic and Social Affairs/Population Division, 2019). As a result, India's population increased from 69.2% to 99.0% of China's population. At the same time, while China's percentage of the world's population has decreased from 21.5% in 1950 to 18.1% in 2020, India's percentage of the world's population has increased from 14.9% in 1950 to 17.9% in 2020.

Socioeconomic development variables such as economic growth, urbanization, education, and women's status have affected population changes differently in China and India; however, the population control policies that have been adopted by the two governments have directly affected population changes. This chapter compares population control policies and their implementations in the two societies.

Accordingly, this chapter compares the following: First, the first-generation leaders' perspectives on population in China and India; second, the population control policies development in different periods in the two countries; and third, the population control policies adopted by the Chinese and Indian governments. Then, I will compare the two societies' policy implementations. Finally, the chapter summarizes and discusses the findings.

A Comparison of First-Generation Leader Perspectives on Population

Since China and India established their governments in the late 1940s after many years of revolutionary wars or independence movements, first-generation leaders, such as Mao Zedong and Deng Xiaoping in China and Mahatma Gandhi and Jawaharlal Nehru in India, possessed extraordinary influence on their societies. Therefore, their perspectives on population had a fundamental impact not only on the adoption of the population control policies but also on the implementations of the policies.

DOI: 10.4324/9781003307419-4

In China, Mao Zedong, the chairman of the Central Committee of the Chinese Communist Party between 1935 and 1976 set the tone for China's population control policies and policy implementations between the 1950s and 1970s. Deng Xiaoping, a vice premier of China between 1950 and 1965 and the actual leader of China between 1978 and 1997, fundamentally influenced the Chinese government's population control policies between the 1980s and 2010s. In India, Mahatma Gandhi, the primary leader of India's independence movement strongly influenced India's population perspectives during the 1940s and 1950s. Jawaharlal Nehru, a leader of India's nationalist movement and the first prime minister of India—he served between 1947 and 1964—fundamentally influenced India's population control policies and their implementations between the 1950s and 1970s. Although his influence declined after the 1970s, Nehru's idea of controlling population to promote economic development has remained with the Indian government up to this point.

Mao's dialectical analysis assumes that anything has two sides, a positive side and a negative side. When one side is considered primary, the other side may be considered secondary. Therefore, Mao always took both the positive and negative sides into consideration when he analyzed social issues. Although he recognized the potential negative impact of the huge Chinese population on socioeconomic development in China, Mao perceived it as secondary in comparison with the positive impact it may have on socioeconomic development. He believed that a huge and rapidly increasing population was a positive factor in China's socioeconomic development. However, each of the two aspects of China's population may develop into its opposite over time. During the 1950s, Mao perceived the rapidly increasing population after the establishment of the new China was a good indicator of China's successful socialism.

Therefore, Mao believed that of all things in the world, people were the most precious. On the other hand, Mao also stated that China's population should grow according to plan and people needed to practice family planning (Tian, 2009). As a result, China developed family planning programs before the 1970s, but they were never earnestly implemented nationwide. After China's population reached 830 million in 1970, Mao perceived that the negative effect of the population had become primary and issued a strong instruction for population control, which led to the nationwide implementation of China's "later marriage" policy. Consequently, China's population growth reduced considerably.

Deng was a pragmatic person, and his focus was on economic development. As a vice premier between 1950 and 1965, Deng supported family planning and population control in China. However, his perspective was often overshadowed by Mao's. Starting in 1954, the Chinese government began to pay attention to the negative side of its population and gradually developed family planning programs. Deng supported these programs, but the implementation of the programs fluctuated between the 1950s and the 1960s. When Deng became the actual leader of China in 1978, he was strongly influenced by Western perspectives on population and perceived China's population as an obstacle to rapid economic development. Deng wanted to raise per capita GDP and reduce China's population growth. Therefore, controlling population growth became China's developmental strategy. He believed that the population was the most difficult thing to handle for China and it must be dealt with strategically (Guo, 2000). Accordingly, the Chinese government adopted the restrictive one-birth-per-couple policy to control population growth.

In India, Western perspectives on population, which assumed that a large population would affect economic development adversely and must be controlled for economic development, failed to influence Gandhi, although he was educated in England (Wang, 2019). His perspective on population was philosophical and based on the concepts of social affection, non-possession, and trusteeship (Davan and Lutz, 1985). Gandhi did not believe that a large population would be a problem. He assumed that once a new social order was created and society developed its own terms of reference, it would adjust itself and find its own solution to population growth problems. Gandhi did not think it was necessary to have one or two isolated and narrowly defined interventions (Ranjan, 1999). In fact, he was against the use of contraceptives, which he considered an insult to womanhood (Mahatma Gandhi Media and Research Service, 2019). Although he had a strong influence in India and his perspective on population affected the implementation of family planning programs, his influence gradually declined after his assassination in 1948.

In contrast with Gandhi, Nehru was less idealistic and more practical on the population problem facing India. Nehru believed that the Industrial Revolution and the spread of modern technology promoted population increase in Europe. An eastward sweep of modern technology would result in a substantial population increase. Huge populations in China and India were a burden and weakness unless they were properly and productively organized. Therefore, India would be better off with fewer people (Nehru, 2004). When he became the prime minister of India, his ideas, as early as in 1952, about population formed a fundamental setting for the adoption of population control policy in India (Ranjan, 1999).

There were similarities between China and India. Both Mao and Gandhi possessed more traditional wisdom, both had some kind of philosophical perspectives on population, and both had positive perceptions of their huge populations. While Mao regarded people as the most precious thing in the world, Gandhi believed that an increase in population was not and ought not to be regarded as a calamity. When Mao thought revolution and production would enable China to feed its population (Mao, 1991), Gandhi believed that with a proper land system and better agriculture and supplementary industry, India would be able to support twice its population (Ranjan, 1999).

Similarly, both Deng and Nehru were more receptive to Western perspectives on population, and both were highly practical and believed that effective control of the population was absolutely necessary for economic development. In China and India, Deng and Nehru's pragmatism affected population control policies more fundamentally.

There were also differences in influence between first-generation leaders in China and India. While Mao supported family planning, Gandhi was against the use of any kind of contraceptives. When Mao believed that family planning would be conducive to woman's health and their development in China, Gandhi considered contraception immoral and damaging to individuals and the nation (Srinivasan, 2017). Another difference was that Mao and Deng were much younger than Gandhi and Nehru. Mao, born 24 years after Gandhi, lived until 1976. Similarly, Deng lived until 1997 and his influence lasted much longer than that of Nehru, who died in 1964. Both Mao and Deng lived about three decades longer than Gandhi and Nehru after the establishments of their new governments. Therefore, they influenced China's population control policies much longer than did Gandhi and Nehru in India. As a result, China's population control started later than India's. China's population control policies were more restrictive and implemented more effectively than India's.

Still another fundamental difference between China and India is that both Mao and Deng were revolutionary leaders who led China's revolution that started from or deeply affected the grassroots level of Chinese society. Contrary to Mao and Deng, Gandhi and Nehru were lawyers educated in Britain, and they started the independence movement mostly from the upper levels of Indian society. Therefore, while Gandhi and Nehru were more likely to elaborate their population perspectives and policies, Mao and Deng were more effective in implementing population control policies.

Although Nehru's perspective on population in India and Deng's on China fundamentally affected population control in the two nations, they more narrowly defined their perspectives on population. Gandhi's and Mao's perspectives on population were less partial, and they refused to be limited by old (or new) Malthusian perspectives on the relationship between population and natural resources. When people focus their attention on population control or sustainable development at present, they may support Deng's and Nehru's contributions to population controls in China and India. However, when people pay attention to human development in the long run, they may feel that Mao and Gandhi have a better understanding of society.

A Comparison of Population Control Policy Developments

Although both the Chinese and Indian governments adopted population control policies, each country's policies have experienced different periods of development. Generally speaking, China's population control policies have developed over five periods. The first period was between 1949 and 1953 during which the Chinese government policy was to limit family planning, the use of contraceptives, and abortion. The second period, between 1954 and 1970, saw the Chinese government gradually develop family planning programs. The programs, however, were implemented neither consistently nor nationwide. During the later 1950s, family planning programs were designed mostly to improve women's personal and family lives. During the 1960s, the programs sought to reduce population growth but were not persistently implemented.

During the third period, between 1971 and 1979, China adopted the later marriage policy. Although the policy was voluntary, it reduced the birth rate and the natural increase rate. During the fourth period, between 1980 and 2015, the government adopted a restrictive one-birth-per-couple policy, which was implemented peremptorily and sometimes coercively. The fifth period started in 2016 when the Chinese government adopted a two-children-per-couple policy, which allows any married couples to have two children. The major purpose of this new policy was to improve the age and gender structures of China's population when population control continues. In 2021, this policy was further relaxed to three children per couple to reverse the lower birth rate trend in China.

In India, population control policies can be roughly divided into three periods. During the first, a service-providing policy period between 1952 and 1961, the government developed a "family limitation and population control" program. Accordingly, the government provided services, devices, and information for family planning but demand for the services was not high.

The second period was between 1962 and March 1977 during which the policy changed gradually into an imperative and target-oriented population control policy. During this period, the Indian government imperiously promoted the use of condoms, diaphragms, jelly, intrauterine contraceptive devices, and sterilization. It also set targets, used different measures to reach the targets, and sometimes forced sterilizations to control population growth. Although the targets were seldom reached, forced sterilization and other policy implementations caused much anger. Eventually, the government was forced to revise the population control policies and their implementations after the ruling party was voted out in the 1977 election.

The third period started in April 1977 when the Indian government's population control policies became part of the family welfare program—it maintained its population control strategy, though. The implementation of the new policies became decentralized, the goals of population control loosened, and the quotations and specific goals for population control were mostly abandoned. Therefore, this is also known as a voluntary population control.

There are many differences in the development of population control policies between the two countries. While the Chinese government changed its perception of continued population growth from positive to negative in the 1950s, the Indian government was unwavering in its perception that the mushrooming growth in the Indian population was an obstacle to socioeconomic development. The Chinese government gave up limiting the use of contraceptives and abortion around 1954 and allowed its citizens access to family planning. The Indian government continued in its ways, popularizing and promoting family planning.

Between the 1960s and 1970s, China's population control policies developed from a general call for family planning to a more aggressive policy that promoted later marriage and birth, longer intervals between births, and fewer children among married couples. The Indian government population control policy changed from a general call for family planning between 1952 and 1961 to quota-directed restrictive population control, that is, from service providing to enforcing the use of contraceptives and sterilizations.

After April 1977, the Indian government did not only give up the coercive measures, but also most of the targets of the population control. When India relaxed its population control after 1977, the Chinese government adopted the most restrictive one-birth-per-couple policy in 1980. When China relaxed its population control in

2016, its birth rate has already been below the replacement level at 1.3 children per woman. However, when India relaxed its population control policy in 1977, its birth rate was at 3.7 children per woman, and it continued its slow but declining trend.

At certain points, China and India shared similar approaches and ideas about the role of population growth in overall development. At times, both nations considered their enormous populations as a burden on their socioeconomic developments; both felt that population control would be conducive to their badly needed socioeconomic developments. While China started its economic reforms in the late 1970s, India began its economic reforms in the early 1990s. Yet when the Chinese government started its economic reform, it tightened population control. When the Indian government embarked on economic reform, the government further relaxed its population control.

It seems that China and India had different perceptions of their population during the 1950s, which may be partially attributed to the death of Gandhi. Had Gandhi not been assassinated, his perspectives on population could have influenced the Indians' perspectives on population. Although both China and India eventually considered population control as a strategic step to further their socioeconomic development, each adopted and enforced a different population control policy and implemented it differently. China's implementation seems much more effective than India's, while India's implementation seems more limited by its societal conditions.

A Comparison of Population Control Policies

Looking at population control policies in China and India enables us to understand the two countries' similarities and differences. It may also help us understand why a policy is effective or not. Since the first two periods of China's population control policies between 1950 and 1970 were either not for population control or not actually implemented, it is inappropriate to compare them with India's population control policies.

Therefore, the third period of China's population control policy or China's initial period of population control policy between 1971 and 1979 will be compared with the first period of India's population control policy, or India's initial population control period policy between 1952 and 1961. A second comparison will be made between China's tightened population control policy implemented from 1980 to 2015 and India's tightened population control policy between 1962 and March 1977. A third comparison will be made between the relaxed population control policy in China since 2016 with the relaxed population control policy in India since April 1977. It is necessary, however, to point out that China relaxed its population control when its birth rate had fallen below the replacement level while India relaxed its population control when the government was voted out.

China and India's population control policies have gone through three periods of development: an initial period, a tightening period, and a relaxed period. India initiated, tightened, and relaxed its population control policies earlier than did China. The developments, impacts, and changes in population control policies in the two societies were different. Table 4.1 provides examples of major population control policies implemented in China and India during these three periods.

Table 4.1 Examples of Major Population Control Policies in China and India

Population Control Policy of China	*Population Control Policy of India* ***
*Initial Period: 1971–1979**	*Initial Period: 1952–1961*
1. In 1971, the government promoted family planning in urban and densely populated rural areas. 2. In 1973, the government popularized the "later marriage and birth, longer intervals between births and fewer children" policy. This meant that males and females would get married 3 years later than the age stipulated by the Marriage Law, wait for 2 years to bear children, have at least a 3-year interval between births, and have two children per couple for urban and densely populated rural areas. 3. In 1978, the government confirmed the "later marriage" policy and specified that fewer means the best is to have one and the maximum number is to have two children for each married couple.	1. According to the First Five-Year Plan, the Indian government should present a clear picture of the factors contributing to the rapid population increase in India; discover suitable techniques of family planning and devise methods by which knowledge of these techniques could be widely disseminated; and give advice on family planning as an integral part of the service of government hospitals and public agencies. 2. It emphasized the use of natural devices for family planning. 3. The goal was to reduce the birth rate to the extent necessary to stabilize the population to a level consistent with the requirements of the national economy.
Tightening Period: 1980–2015	*Tightening Period: 1962–March 1977*
1. One birth per couple in urban and densely populated rural areas. 2. Limit China's total population to 1.2 billion while quadrupling its GNP by 2,000. 3. Families with difficulties may have two children. 4. Minimum age for marriage was increased in 1980: For males, it increased from 20 to 22, and for females, it increased from 18 to 20.	1. The Third Five-Year Plan (1961–1966) goal was to reduce the birth rate to 2.5% by 1972. 2. The Fourth Five-Year Plan (1969–1974) goal was to reduce the national birth rate to 3.2% by 1974 and further to 2.5% within 10–12 years, and have 14.9 million sterilizations. 3. The Fifth Five-Year Plan (1974–1979) goal was to reduce the birth rate to 3% by 1979 and to 2.5% by 1984. 4. The sterilization for both men and women was adopted. 5. All kinds of birth control methods were encouraged. 6. In 1971, the government adopted the Medical Termination of Pregnancy Act to allow for abortions performed by a medical practitioner within the first 3 months of pregnancy, except in the states of Jammu and Kashmir, both of which are mostly inhabited by Muslims. 7. Minimum age for marriage was increased: For males, it increased from 18 to 21, and for females, it increased from 15 to 18. 8. The number of MPs and MLAs was fixed till the year 2001 on the basis of the census of 1971. 9. Forced sterilization was permitted.

(*Continued*)

Table 4.1 (Continued)

Population Control Policy of China	*Population Control Policy of India* ***
Relaxed Period: Since 2016 **	*Relaxed Period: Since April 1977*
1. Two-children-per-couple policy to improve the gender and age structure of the population in 2016. 2. Three-children-per-couple policy to improve the gender and age structure of the population in 2021.	1. The Six Five-Year Plan (1980–1985) long-term goals were to reduce the average family size from 4.2 children in 1979 to 2.3 and reduce the birth rate from 3.3% in 1978 to 2.1% by 2001 and reduce the death rate from 1.4% in 1978 to 0.9% and reduce the infant mortality rate from 129 to 60 or less by 2001. The short-term goals were to carry out 22 million sterilizations, have 22 million IUDs inserted, and increase the number of users of condoms, oral contraceptives, and other conventional methods to 11 million in the period of 1984–1985. 3. The National Population Policy 2000 included three major goals: The temporary objective was to provide birth control devices and to develop a health protection framework and recruit health workers to participate in family planning. The mid-term objective was to bring down the total fertility rate to a replacement level of 2.1 by 2010. The long-term objective was to achieve population stabilization by 2045. The population has to be stabilized at the level which must be harmonious from the points of view of economic and social development and environmental protection.

Sources:

* China Development Research Foundation. 2012. China Development Report 2011/12, the Change of the Population and the Adjustment of Population Policy. Beijing: China Development Press.

** Xin Hua News Website, 2016. The Decision of the Central Committee of the Chinese Communist Party and the State Council of China on the Implementation of the Two-Children-Per-Couple Policy Nationwide and on the Reformation and Improvement of the Management and Services of Family Planning. Retrieved on April 17, 2020, at www.xinhuanet.com//politics/2016-01/05/c_1117678260.htm.

*** Srinivasan, Krishnamurthy. 2017. Population Concerns in India: Shifting Trends, Policies, and Programs. New Delhi: Sage.

China's policy during the initial population control period between 1971 and 1979 was specific and directly affected families. It asked the Chinese to get married 3 years later than the marriage law age of 20 for males and 18 for females. Besides later marriage, the policy asked each married couple to bear a child 2 years after marriage. The policy also asked married couples to have a 3-year interval between two births and to stop after a maximum of two children.

Different from China, India's initial population control policy between 1952 and 1961 focused on understanding its population and providing information, advice, and services to married couples. None of the policies sought to control population growth directly. Their general goal was to reduce the birth rate to the extent necessary to stabilize the population at a level consistent with the requirements of the national economy (Srinivasan, 2017).

The initial Chinese population control policy was aimed at families and worked on delaying marriages, reducing the number of childbirth for each married couple and limiting each married couple to two children. In contrast, India's initial population control policy focused on understanding the issue and providing advice and services. The government's goal was general and unspecific.

There were also fundamental differences in the population control policies between the two nations when the Chinese (1980–2015) and Indian governments (1962–1977) tightened their population controls. In China, the government adopted a development strategy to limit its population to 1.2 billion and quadruple its GNP by 2000. At the same time, the government adopted a one-birth-per-couple policy, which was specific and restrictive. Although not every family followed the policy in China, most of the Han majority living in urban areas or densely populated rural areas followed it.

Contrary to China, India's population control policy did not directly limit childbirths by families. For example, during the Fourth Five-Year Plan period between 1969 and 1974, the Indian government enforced its population control by setting its goals to reduce the national birth rate to 32 per thousand by 1974 and further to 25 per thousand within 10–12 years. At the same time, the government policy expected to have 14.9 million sterilizations. During the emergency period between 1975 and 1977, the Indian government set a goal of reducing the nation's birth rate to 30 per thousand by 1979 and 25 per thousand by 1984 or bring down the national natural increase rate to 14 per thousand by 1984 (Srinivasan, 2017). Although sterilizations were vigorously carried out and a great number had been completed, sterilization did not always turn out to be effective in population control, for "the Motto of an average India couple seems to have as many children as desired and then go for sterilization" (Srinivasan, 2017: 89).

In order to tighten their population control, both China and India increased the minimum age for marriage. China increased the minimum marriage age to 20 for females and 22 for males in 1980 and the marriage law was vigorously enforced. As a result, child marriage is rare in China. Similarly, India increased the minimum marriage age to 18 for females and 21 for males in 1978. The Indian government enforced the law vigorously and even punished those who married a child, who performed a child marriage ceremony, or who were parents or guardians of a person who took part in the child marriage. However, about 47% of females still got married by the age of 18 between 2005 and 2006 (UNICEF, 2020). Obviously, it is much more difficult for the Indian government to enforce the laws than the Chinese government. Similarly, it is more difficult for the Indian government to implement the population control policies in India.

In comparison, China's policy aimed at each individual family while India's policy aimed at the national birth rate. China's policy is more direct and more specific; therefore, more effective in controlling the population growth, for when each family's number of births has been reduced, the fall of the national increase rate will follow. On the Indian side, however, the policy is more indirect and less specific. When India's policy aimed at the national increase rate and the method was to increase sterilizations, it was not only indirect but also ineffective, for when more sterilizations are performed on those who no longer want children, more sterilizations do not actually mean fewer births. While both nations revised their marriage laws to increase their marriage age, India was unable to effectively enforce the marriage law.

During the relaxed population control period in China and India, there was a fundamental difference between China and India. China relaxed its population control policy in 2016 because its birth rate had already fallen below the replacement level and there was a strong need to adjust its gender and age structures. In contrast, India relaxed its policy in 1977 because its ruling party was voted out. While China adopted a two-children-per-couple policy in 2016 and a three-children-per couple policy in 2021, the Indian government merged its population control policy into the family welfare programs or disguised its population control within the family welfare programs after 1977 when the population was still growing rapidly.

Even when the Indian government's population control policy pushed to reduce the number of children married couples could have, the specific goal was deemphasized by other specific goals, such as reductions in the death rate or increases in sterilizations and condom users. Similarly, when the Indian government set fixed targets on the number of contraceptive users for the family planning workers, the targets did not directly affect each family's childbirth nor did it directly affect population growth rates.

India's National Population Policy 2000 remains indirect and unspecific. The new policy included three major objectives. The temporary objective was to provide birth control devices, develop health protection frameworks, and recruit health workers to participate in family planning. The mid-term objective was to lower the total fertility rate to a replacement level of 2.1 by 2010. The long-term objective was to achieve population stabilization by 2045.

These comparisons indicate that China's population control policies were often more specific, more directly targeted families, and consequently were more effective in reducing China's population growth. On the contrary, Indian population control policies were less specific, less directly targeted families, and were, therefore, less effective. In other words, Chinese population control policies mostly focused on ends while the Indian population control policies mostly worked on means. Although some states in India have a two-children-per-couple policy, most of Indian society rejects the policy.

Of course, these population control policy differences are determined mostly by the social conditions in the two different societies. It is the social conditions that determine what kind of policy a society can adopt and how the policy can be implemented. For example, when legislator, Prahalad Singh Patel, proposed a two-children-per-couple policy in India, in 2016, many Indians thought it was inappropriate for the nation; a few Indian states have implemented such a policy, though.

A Comparison of Policy Implementations

In developing countries like China and India, it was not easy to motivate a large number of uneducated people, especially farmers in rural areas, to practice family planning during the 1970s and 1980s. Therefore, China and India have established multi-level population control organizations, utilized different methods to disseminate information about family planning, and employed different incentives and disincentives to implement the population control policies.

In China, well-organized family planning commissions have been set up at all levels of society. For example, in the 1970s and 1980s, such commissions were comprised of party officers, demographers, doctors, and women cadres. At the national level, there was a Family Planning Commission under the State Council. This agency was responsible for the implementation of policies relating to family planning and for supervising and guiding the family planning programs at provincial and lower levels. When a new State Family Planning Commission was established in March 1981, Vice Premier Chen Muhua was in charge. Under this commission, there was a national family planning center for publicizing the policy, educating the family planning program staff, and incorporating relevant technology, and training personnel. In addition to this center, there was a Family Planning Scientific Research Institute that carried out technical research on family planning and provided technical advice to the State Family Planning Commission.

At the provincial level, there were family planning commissions, the functions of which were to oversee the provincial family planning offices. Each office had its own supervisory and fieldworkers who worked in coordination with provincial health departments. These provincial departments provided technical support for family planning programs through local facilities and personnel. Offices at this level were responsible for formulating local policy, directing policy implementation, maintaining contraceptive supplies, conducting research on and evaluating new contraceptives, and collecting statistics on planned births. Throughout China, there were 29 such units at the provincial level, consisting of 21 provinces, five autonomous regions, and three centrally administered municipalities.

At the county level and with the guidance of the local family planning commission, family planning offices directed the local programs. These offices coordinated the family planning activities of the county health departments, hospitals, and mass organizations involved in family planning work. County medical facilities and personnel and the staff of the local health clinics at the neighborhood level in urban areas and the commune and brigade levels in rural areas were also expected to provide support for family planning work.

At the grassroots level, at almost every urban unit, there was a family planning worker or a volunteer who worked especially for the unit, be it a school, a neighborhood, or a factory workshop. In the rural areas, there were barefoot doctors who worked in the production brigades. Whether a family planning worker or barefoot doctor, this person was the neighbor of the urbanites or the villagers with whom he or she worked. Thus, he or she knew quite well who should be talked to about family planning or who needed contraceptives. With the strong support of the Party, the government, and the authority of every unit, the commissions, family planning workers, and barefoot doctors worked zealously to make China's population control program a success.

These grassroots family planning workers worked to convey the government's policy and ensure people follow policy. During the 1980s, thousands of medical workers, party secretaries, and women cadres were mobilized to explain the one-birth-per-couple policy to the people. They told people about the scarcity of the country's natural resources which made family planning necessary; they demonstrated the significance of family planning for the country as well as for themselves; and they persuaded people to follow the policy strictly.

Information about family planning not only was delivered by cadres orally but also appeared in newspapers, on television, and in magazines. Many newspaper and magazine articles told people that their individual prosperity depended on modernizing the country—a goal which could only be realized when population growth decreased. Women cadres often told young mothers that with more children, they could not afford to bring their children up healthily and well-educated. What was more, women were told that having many children would deprive them of their status equal to men. Too many children would decrease a mother's educational opportunity and work time, both of which were essential to achieve equal rights. In villages and communes, loudspeakers provided family planning messages along with music and educational features. In urban areas, family planning messages were frequent. Everywhere, these messages were repeated through posters that stressed the happy family size—father, mother, and one child.

Family planning information also offered detailed advice about all kinds of contraceptive devices which were made available, free of charge, to married couples. These included such things as pills, condoms, intrauterine contraceptive devices, and sterilization operations. All drug stores and family offices throughout the country provided birth control devices. Very often, contraceptives were even delivered to the homes of married couples. If a woman suspected contraceptive failure, she was expected to visit a doctor for a diagnosis of pregnancy. If the tests were positive, and she did not want to have a baby, an abortion was always available. Having an abortion entitled a woman to a paid vacation, as did a contraceptive sterilization operation (Population Reference Bureau, 1979).

In India, family planning organizations have existed for a long time and these organizations engaged in all kinds of family planning work, including information dissemination and carrying out government family planning programs. For example, family planning programs were centrally sponsored in India in the 1970s, meaning the central government reimbursed state governments for about 100 percent of their expenditures. Like in China, India's family planning program was also integrated into the general medical and health bureaucracy and was present at all levels of the government.

At the national level, there was a Department of Family Planning which was part of the Ministry of Health and Family Planning. This central ministry had a major role in shaping the overall family planning programs. By using its financial powers, the ministry set goals for the number of sterilizations it would perform, determined information and educational strategies, established staffing patterns, and determined patterns of fund allocation. However, in India there were no powerful organizations like the family planning commissions in China that could rally the support from the ruling party and the government.

At the state level, there were 21 state family planning bureaus in the 1970s. The state family planning officer headed the State Family Bureau which was a separate entity within the Directorate with special responsibility for the state's family planning program. This officer was assisted by deputy and assistant directors who were in charge of divisions in the bureau, such as training, mass education, propaganda, and administration. Unable to control the block extension educator and the health visitors in the rural family planning programs, the officer in charge of family planning at the state level had limited power, conditions quite different from those of China.

At the district level, there were 327 family planning bureaus. Before 1973, the district family planning program was divided into a rural and an urban component. The urban program was administered by the civil surgeon, a physician from the state medical service. His primary responsibility in family planning was for urban areas; however, he might also give technical guidance to medical officers in rural primary centers, countersign the District Medical Officer of Health's personnel evaluations, and certify medical officers to perform vasectomies and other surgery (Simmons and Ashraf, 1978).

The District Medical Officer of Health, a physician from the State Health Service, who was in charge of district public health activities, was in charge of rural family planning programs. He controlled the rural primary health centers in his district, helped the medical officers and their staff, and compiled family planning statistics. After 1973, rural and urban activities were combined under one authority. The chief medical officer of health was responsible for all health, medical, and family planning activities in the district.

Below the district level, there were 1,879 family welfare planning centers in urban areas, and 5,201 family welfare planning centers and 32,423 sub-centers in rural areas. The urban centers were typically staffed by a physician and one or two paramedical personnel. Each of these centers covered a population of about 50,000. The rural centers were staffed by one or two physicians and two or three paramedical personnel, and each covered a population of about 100,000. Under each of these centers, there were still about six sub-centers, each of which covered a population of about 10,000 to 15,000. In addition to those official organizations, there were 8,000 non-governmental agencies supported by government grants (Jain, 1975). The sub-centers were scattered in rural areas with staff members responsible for carrying out family planning in their working area.

Similar to China's family planning programs, the Indian government also put great effort into its propaganda. To implement its family planning policy:

> Several activities for disseminating information and heightening awareness of family planning and small family concepts are organized and coordinated by the mass education media divisions at the central, state, and district levels. Extensive use is made of such mass media as radio, press, and film as well as of such traditional media as wall paintings; posters on buses, railway

> engines, and in post offices; match box labels; and billboards. In addition, mobile publicity units and the song and drama division of the Ministry of Information and Broadcasting also try to arouse interest in and disseminate information about family planning. These activities are supplemented, reinforced, and supported by person-to-person contact and group meetings.
> (Jain, 1975: 253)

In their population control efforts, both governments in China and India have established extensive policy implementation organizations, from the central government to the grassroots level. Those organizations worked diligently in both the Chinese and Indian societies to popularize family planning information, promote family planning, advise families that need family planning, and distribute family planning devices.

A careful examination, however, reveals some important differences. One difference is that the family planning commissions are present at all levels of the government, including the central, provincial, and county-level government in China, but not in India. The Chinese family planning commissions were closely associated with the Communist Party, the government, and all kinds of authorities and organizations in China. Those commissions provided strong support from a number of organizations at political, administrative, productive, and voluntary levels. However, in India, those family planning officials are often secondary to other government organizations and are disabled by a lack of power and support from other organizations in the society. Sometimes, the family planning organizations' efforts are canceled out by other government organizations.

Another fundamental difference between China and India is that in China there are always some women cadres at each family planning and policy implementation level. These women cadres have played an important role in family planning, both in giving advice and in persuading mothers to practice birth control. In India, however, women do not always have an equal status to men and are not fully mobilized to take part in family planning education. When women's power diminished, the effectiveness of family planning programs was reduced.

Still another difference affecting population control is that in India there are not enough workers who can work efficiently among farmers. Moreover, these fieldworkers are often viewed as outsiders by the Indian villagers. As a result, they cannot work as effectively as those family planning workers in China who are members of the villages or working organizations.

The problems with the Indian organization of family planning are quite complicated. As Indian Professor Misra and his associates have pointed out:

> One may list a whole array of conditions that ought to be changed in order to improve that organizational context, but such stipulations tended to go far beyond the existing potential for change. Efforts to implement the family planning program in India are constrained by the fact that the organizational capacity does not exist to bring about maximally effective interactions between clients and field workers. The condition that strained the program

> from translating the ideas behind the extension strategy into actual ongoing behavior on the part of the field staff strike at the very foundations of not only the medical and health system but also the general bureaucracy and the political and economic system of which they were an integral part.
>
> (Misra, 1976: 73)

In spreading the ideas of family planning, the governments of both China and India have endeavored to utilize television, films, posters, newspapers, and magazines. The difference is that the Chinese government has been able to mobilize a large number of people to criticize the traditional beliefs that hinder family planning and persuade people to accept the idea of family planning as well as actually put it into practice by providing adequate contraceptives for those who need them and promising to take care of the aged. The Indian government, on the other hand, can neither mobilize many people to criticize the religious beliefs that influence family planning nor persuade most people to practice family planning. In addition, India's health care system cannot provide every married couple adequate contraception free of charge nor can the economic system promise to support old people. When taking the whole issue of population control into consideration, it becomes obvious that both the Chinese and Indian governments have tried their best, but the different social conditions cause different results.

Both the Chinese and Indian governments utilized incentives and disincentives in their population control policy implementations. For example, the one-child policy was backed by social sanctions in China. If parents who had one child agreed not to have more children, they would get a cash reward each month until their child was 16 years old. Such a cash reward often equaled approximately one-tenth of an average income in the early 1980s and was enough to pay for a three-person family's house rent, electricity, and water at that time. In some areas, the one-child parents enjoyed other privileges, such as better housing or extra holidays. Organizations even rewarded the one-child parents who first had sterilization operations with bikes, sewing machines, or television sets. During the early 1980s, such rewards were significant for most families. But if those parents later changed their minds and decided to have a second child, they would not only have to return all the rewards to the government but also be punished by reprimand or fine. In fact, parents who had a third child sometimes lost their jobs.

Through all these efforts, people were greatly influenced, and the one-child family had become an accepted social norm during the 1990s and 2010s in China. Consequently, many people followed the one-birth-per-couple policy automatically and applied strong pressure on those who did not want to comply. In the cities, most young couples simply took the one-birth-per-couple policy for granted and believed that having only one child was good for them. In the countryside, some couples insisted on having more than one child, but most people were satisfied with one, even if they would like to have had more. Many agreed that, for the development of the country, the one-birth-per-couple policy was a necessity.

India had considerable experience with a variety of incentive programs designed to influence individual reproductive behavior. The first such large-scale incentive scheme was begun in 1956 by the state of Madras. Selected private medical practitioners received a subsidy of Rs. 25 per case to perform vasectomies on low-income men. Subsequently, a cash grant of Rs. 30 was awarded to every poor person who agreed to be sterilized. From 1959, the sum of Rs. 10 was paid to canvassers and tutors in family planning who sent persons for sterilization to approved surgeons and government hospitals. Incentive programs involving direct cash payments to users, motivators, and service providers were soon instituted throughout India (David, 1982).

Although such incentives were effective in some areas, they are not effective in others. In 1976, when the Indian government tried to enhance its population programs, incentives increased, and, in some areas, factory workers and servants were not only lured but also threatened to be dismissed if they did not agree to sterilization. Some who refused to accept sterilization were actually suspended from their jobs for 7 or 8 days, others reported having their salaries withheld for 3 to 4 months. When the sterilization campus reopened in 1982, the rewards increased to about $22 to females and $15 to males (Stolc, 2008).

Although both governments utilized incentives and disincentives to promote their population control policies, Chinese incentives seemed greater, lasted longer, and were more effective than the one-time incentives offered in India. "The incentive programs in India have comprised mostly one-time awards for acceptance of long-term birth control methods that do not cover the economic impact that an additional child could have had in a family's life" (Stolc, 2008: 22).

A Comparison of Policy Effectiveness

As a result of the different population control policies and policy implementations, population changes have occurred differently in China and India. During the initial population control period between 1971 and 1979, China's total fertility reduced from 5.43 to 2.91, a 46% reduction. In comparison, India's total fertility reduced from 5.90 to 5.89 during the initial population control period between 1952 and 1961, a reduction of about 0.2%. Similarly, China's birth rate during the initial period between 1971 and 1979 reduced from 3.07% to 1.78% while India's birth rate during the initial period between 1952 and 1961 reduced from 4.42% to 4.18%. When China's birth rate fell 42%, India's birth rate declined 5.4%. Consequently, China's natural increase rate reduced from 2.33% in 1971 to 1.16% in 1979 while India's natural increase rate increased from 1.61% in 1952 to 2.02% in 1961. While China's natural increase rate declined 50%, India's increased 25% during the initial population control period. China's initial period of population control was much more effective than that of India.

During the tightened population control period from 1980 to 2015, China's total fertility reduced from 2.81 to 1.66, a 41% reduction. In comparison, India's total fertility reduced from 5.89 to 5.06 during the tightened population control period between 1962 and 1977, a decline of 14%. Similarly, China's birth rate during the tightened population control period between 1980 and 2015 reduced from 1.82% to 1.20% while India's birth rate during the tightened period between 1962 and 1977 fell from 4.16% to 3.70%. When China's birth rate further reduced 34%, India's birth rate reduced 11%. Consequently, China's natural increase rate reduced from 1.19% in 1980 to 0.49% in 2015 while India's natural increase rate increased from 2.05% in 1962 to 2.32% in 1977. When the natural increase rate declined 59% in China, India's natural increase rate increased 13% during the tightened population control period. During the tightened population control period, China's population control policy was much more effective than India's. While China's tightened population control reduced its population growth, India's population was growing even more rapidly during the tightened population control period.

During the relaxed population control period from 2016 to 2020, China's total fertility increased slightly from 1.67 to 1.70, which was a weak 1.8% increase. In comparison, India's total fertility reduced from 4.97 to 2.18 during the relaxed population control period between 1978 and 2021, and the reduction was 56%. Similarly, China's birth rate after the adoption of the relaxed policy in 2015 continued to fall from 1.36% in 2016 to 0.85%, a birth rate decline in China of 37.5%, while India's birth rate diminished from 3.67% in 1978 to 1.76% in 2020, a reduction of 52%. Consequently, China's natural increase rate further reduced from 0.65% in 2016 to 0.15% in 2020 while India's natural increase rate reduced from 2.31% in 1978 to 0.99% in 2020. When the natural increase rate further reduced 77% in China, India's natural increase rate reduced 57% during the relaxed population control period. It was during the relaxed period that India's total fertility and birth rate fell more than half that of China. It seems that China's relaxed population control had not yet reversed the population growth trend.

Taking seven decades of population growth into consideration, it is obvious that China's population has fallen much more rapidly than India's. Between 1950 and 2020, China's population increased from about 544 million to about 1,403 million while India's increased from about 376 million to 1,389 million (see Table 4.2). During the same period, India's percentage of China's population has increased from about 69.2% in 1950 to about 99.0% in 2020. While China's percentage of the world's population decreased from about 21.5% in 1950 to about 18.1% in 2020, India's percentage of the world's population increased from about 14.9% in 1950 to about 17.9% in 2020. That means that in the past seven decades, China's population was growing more slowly while India's population was growing faster than that of the world's population.

The data also indicate that China's ten-year increase rate started to decrease when the Chinese government started to implement the population control policies in 1970. And it continued to decrease when the Chinese government tightened its population control policy in 1980. Contrary to China, India's ten-year population increase rate was getting greater when the Indian government started its population control in 1952, and it continued to increase more rapidly when the Indian government tightened its population control in 1962. The ten-year increase rate only started to decrease when the Indian government relaxed its population control policies in 1977. This may indicate that India's population control may have not made much difference in its population growth, and India's population growth may have been affected more by other socioeconomic factors.

Table 4.2 Population Changes in China and India

Year	*China's Total Population*	*Ten-Year Increase*	*China's Percentage of the World's population*	*India's Total Population*	*Ten-Year Increase*	*India's Percentage of the World's Population*	*World's Total Population*	*India's Population Percentage of China*
1950	544,113,000		21.5%	376,325,000		14.9%	2,525,149,000	69.2%
1960	644,450,000	18.4%	21.4%	449,662,000	19.5%	14.9%	3,018,344,000	69.8%
1970	808,511,000	25.5%	22.0%	553,943,000	23.2%	15.0%	3,682,488,000	68.5%
1980	977,837,000	20.9%	22.0%	697,230,000	25.9%	15.7%	4,439,632,000	71.3%
1990	1,154,606,000	18.1%	21.8%	870,602,000	24.9%	16.4%	5,309,668,000	75.4%
2000	1,269,975,000	10.0%	20.7%	1,053,481,000	21.0%	17.2%	6,126,622,000	83.0%
2010	1,340,969,000	5.6%	19.4%	1,230,985,000	16.8%	17.8%	6,929,725,000	91.8%
2020	1,402,848,000	4.6%	18.1%	1,388,859,000	12.8%	17.9%	7,758,157,000	99.0%

Sources: United Nations Department of Economic and Social Affairs/Population Division

World Population Prospects: The 2015 Revision, Volume I: Comprehensive Tables. (Pages: 18–21 Retrieved on January 18, 2017, at https://esa.un.org/unpd/wpp/Publications/Files/WPP2015_Volume-I_Comprehensive-Tables.pdf.

Summary and Discussions

The first-generation leaders in both countries have fundamentally influenced the perceptions of their populations and the adoption and implementation of their population control policies. The leaders have different perspectives on their population; however, it was the leaders, such as Deng and Nehru, who had more practical values and were receptive to Western perspectives on population, affected the population control policies in China and India more fundamentally. Leaders with more traditional ideas, like Mao and Gandhi, perceived population as influenced by social conditions and saw it in a longer historical timeframe. They had a more positive perspective on population and would more likely utilize other policies to address population issues.

Although the Chinese government developed population control policies much later than the Indian government, the factors behind each of the two governments' relaxation of their population control policies were totally different. When the Indian government relaxed its restrictive population control policy in 1977, its population was still growing rapidly. India's birth rate was 3.7%, and the natural increase rate was 2.3% (see Table 3.1). Relaxing India's population control policy was a concession to the ruling party's political opponents and social pressure. When the Chinese government began to relax its restrictive population control policy in 2016, its birth rate was 1.3% and its natural increase rate was 0.6% (see Table 2.1). China's birth rate was below the replacement level in 2016. In relaxing its population control policy, its goal was to improve the nation's gender balance and reduce the aging population's impact on the country.

Compared to the India's control policies, China's control policies were not only much more restrictive but also more specific and directed at families. While Indian policies aimed at reducing the national birth rate and the natural increase rate and making India's demographic profile fit its socioeconomic development, Chinese policies aimed to reduce the number of children per family.

The two governments implemented their population control policies differently although both established similar organizations and employed similar mechanisms to promote their population control policies. The Chinese state established a stronger government organizational system, employed mass media to popularize the policies, and utilized more effective incentives and disincentives to carry out its policy. The Indian government's organizational system was less powerful, its popularization of policies less effective, and the incentives and disincentives less effective. More important, the Chinese were much more responsive to the population control policies than were the Indians.

Policy effectiveness is essential in evaluating population control policies in the two societies. If China had increased its percentage of the world's population as had India between 1950 and 2020 (3% more than in 1950), China would have 24.5% of the world's population in 2020. Then, China's total population would reach 1.9 billion. In other words, China's population control may have averted an additional 500 million people in the world. Had India, in contrast, controlled its population as effectively as China, India would have 3.4% fewer or 11.5% of the world's total population in 2020. Then, India would have had a total population of 892 million instead of 1,389 million in 2020. As we have seen, population control may have contributed more to the socioeconomic development in China than in India during the seven decades between 1950 and 2020 (see Table 4.2).

The less effective population control policies in India, however; will mean its population will continue to grow for many more years. It also means that it will have to face an overpopulation problem for a much longer than China. Accordingly, Indian socioeconomic development will be affected or delayed by its huge population for a longer period of time. Since Indian population control policies have never fundamentally altered natural population growth, the government may not have to take steps to reduce the problem of an aging population any time soon. In the long run, India may actually have a smoother decline in birth rate and natural increase rate than China.

On the other hand, China's more effective population control policies may have cost more than India's did politically, socially, and demographically. For example, India's population control has been criticized much less at home and abroad than China's, whose abrupt decrease in population growth has accelerated its aging. India still has a much younger population. Similarly, China's one-birth-per-couple policy may have damaged family values, which are essential to the functioning of Chinese society.

In the world today, many developed nations have adopted policies to increase population growth while most developing nations are trying to reduce population growth. Demographically, China is at a stage of moving from a developing nation into a developed nation. It may be a good idea for China to further relax its current population control to avoid having to adopt a new policy to encourage population growth in the future. For China, a stable population is more conducive than a shrinking population to stabilize socioeconomic development. As for India, it may be appropriate for the government to continue its efforts in population control and further reduce the growth rate of its huge population.

References

Davan, R. and M. Lutz. 1985. *Essays in Gandhian Economics*. New Delhi: Gandhi Peace Foundation.

David, Henry P. 1982. "Incentives, Reproductive Behavior, and Integrated Community Development in Asia". *Studies in Family Planning* 13: 159–165.

Guo, Weiming. 2000. "A Description of the Research on Deng Xiaoping's Population Thought". *Population Research* 24(6): 66–69.

Jain, Anrudh. 1975. "Family Planning Program: World Review 1974", in *Studies in Family Planning*. New York, NY: The Population Council 6,253.

Mahatma Gandhi Media and Research Service. 2019. "Thus Spake Gandhi, Select Quotations by Mahatma Gandhi, Birth Control. Gandhiserve Foundation". Retrieved on March 22, 2019 from https://www.gandhiservefoundation.org/about-mahatma-gandhi/thus-spake-gandhi/birth-control-1/.

Mao, Zedong. 1991. *Selected Works of Mao Zedong*, Vol. 4. Kunming: People's Press (Second Print by Yunnan People's Press).

Misra, B. D., Ruth Simmons, Ali Ashref and George Simmon. 1976. "The Dilemma of Family Planning in a North Indian State". *Studies in Family Planning* 7 (3): 66–74.

Nehru, J. 2004. *The Discovery of India*. East Rutherford, NJ: Penguin Books.

Population Reference Bureau. 1979. *World Population Growth and Response 1965–1975*. Washington, DC: Population Reference Bureau.

Ranjan, A. 1999. *Population and Development: The Indian Perspective*. Datia: Shyam Institute.

Simmons, Ruth S. and Ali Ashraf. 1978. "Implementing Family Planning in a Ministry of Health: Organizational Barriers at the State and District Levels", in *Studies in Family Planning*. New York, NY: The Population Council 9, 22–34.

Srinivasan, K. 2017. *Population Concerns in India: Shifting Trends, Policies, and Programs*. New Delhi: Sage Publications India Pvt Ltd.

Stolc, Phyllis E. W. 2008. "Seeking Zero Growth: Population Policy in China and India". *Graduate Journal of Asia-Pacific Studies* 6 (2): 10–32.

Tian, Xueyan. 2009. *Sixty Years of Population Policy in China*. Beijing: Social Sciences Press of China.

UNICEF. 2020. "End Child Marriage: India Has the Largest Number of Brides in the World – One-third of the Global Total". *For Every Child, India*. Retrieved on July 1, 2020 from www.unicef.org/india/what-we-do/end-child-marriage.

United Nations Department of Economic and Social Affairs/Population Division, 2019. *World Population Prospects, 2017: The Highlights*. New York, NY: United Nations.

United Nations Department of Economic and Social Affairs/Population Division. 2022. "World Population Prospects 2022, Summary of Results". Retrieved on September 5, 2022 from www.un.org/development/desa/pd/sites/www.un.org.development.desa.pd/files/wpp2022_summary_of_results.pdf.

Wang, Gabe T. 2018. "A Comparison of Population Changes and Social Factors That Have Affected the Population Changes in China and India". *Jiang Su Social Science* 2018 (5): 82–91.

Wang, Gabe T. 2019. "Population Control Policies and Implementations in India". *Journal of Sociology and Social Work* 7 (2): 135–144.

5 Population Change and Economic Development in China and India

Research on the Relationship Between Population and Economic Development

Ever since Malthus published his famous essay on the principles of population in 1798, people have worried that population growth would eventually depress economic development, for land and natural resources are limited while population growth can be unlimited. Although the world's population has grown from one billion in 1798 to eight billion in 2022, the world economy is developing much faster than the growth of the world's population, and human lives in most parts of the world are still improving. Nevertheless, many are still worried about the growth of the world's population and how it may impact economic development.

Accordingly, many researchers have studied the relationship between population growth and economic development (Birdsall et al., 2001; Headey and Hodge, 2009; Huang and Xie, 2013; Yao, Kinugasa, and Hamori, 2013) although empirical research in the 1960s and 1980s did not show correlations between population growth and per capita economic growth (Kuznets, 1966; Simon, 1981).

While some researchers found that population growth and economic development were negatively related (Birdsall and Sinding, 2001; Mason, 2001; Fox and Dyson, 2015), other researchers found that population growth and economic development were positively related. Kuznets (1966, 1973) found that population was the ultimate resource for economic development. Birdsall (1977) saw that population growth could spur demand and the desire to consume and invest and develop technologies and, therefore, positively influenced economic development. Similarly, Simon argued that increasing the number of children did little to lower savings rates, instead constituting an increased labor supply for parents (Simon, 1977). Kremer (1993) also argued that population growth led to technological progress and economic development. As a result, population growth improves living standards in the long term.

Since the 1980s, many researchers found that the decline in population growth among Organization for Economic Co-operation and Development countries

DOI: 10.4324/9781003307419-5

appeared to be slowing economic growth rather than accelerating it. By the late 1990s, a new wave of research on cross-country growth seemed to provide further empirical support for the idea that population growth was positively related to economic growth (Galor and Weil, 2000; Li and Zhang, 2007; Headey and Hodge, 2009; Yao, Kinugasa and Hamori, 2013). More specifically, some found aging populations were negatively related to economic development. If a higher percentage of the population was working age in a society, then the society would enjoy a demographic dividend and economic development would be faster than in a society with a smaller working population (Bloom and Williamson, 1998; Bloom, Canning, and Sevilla, 2003).

While researchers found that population growth and economic development were related to each other, the direction of impact or whether population growth caused economic development or economic development caused population growth was not quite clear. Some found that economic development caused population growth through increasing birth rate or migration (McNicoll, 1984). Others found that economic growth would reduce population growth, for women's increased wages and the rising cost of raising children would reduce fertility (Galor and Weil, 2000).

Still others found that population growth could either directly or indirectly affect economic development. The direct impact of population growth was negative because it leads to lower income per capita. The indirect impact, however, was positive because population growth promotes technological progress, which promotes economic development (Yamaguchi, 1973). Still others found that the relationship between population growth and economic development was different between the developing and the developed nations (Kelly, 2001). According to McNicoll (2006), demographic transition was more likely a result of effective administration, equality, the improvement of health care, education, family planning, adoption of a market economy, and industrialization.

Research also indicated that the relationship between population growth and economic development was highly complicated. Population growth might be either favorable or unfavorable to economic development, depending on where, when, and how it takes place (Kumar, 2021). When population growth was associated with high fertility and an increasing number of children relative to adults, the number of consumers grows more rapidly than the number of producers. Therefore, the burden of dependents on active workers would be greater, and the effect might be negative on economic development. However, when there was a rise in life expectancy that extended the productive years of workers, then the increased burden of dependency might be partially offset.

It seems that research on the relationship between population growth and economic development is not conclusive. Population growth could be positively or negatively related to economic development. The impact of population growth on economic development could be direct or indirect. Similarly, the relationship between population growth and economic development could be different in developed and developing nations.

Population Change and Economic Development in China and India

Since China and India implemented their population control policies with different degrees of effectiveness, India's total population increased much more rapidly than China's. Between 1980 and 2020, China's total population increased from about 987,050,000 to about 1,412,120,000 (see Table 2.1), which is a 43.1% increase within 40 years. During the same period, India's total population increased from about 698,653,000 to about 1,380,004,000 (see Table 3.1), a 97.5% increase within 40 years.

Total fertility rate (TFR) indicates the total number of children that would be born to each woman if she were to live to the end of her childbearing years and give birth to children. Within 40 years, China's TFR decreased from 2.81in 1980 to 1.70 in 2020, a 39.1% decrease. During the same period, India's TFR decreased from 4.86 to 2.20, a 54.1% decrease. Although India's TFR decreased more rapidly than China's, the actual TFR in India was still higher than in China between 1980 and 2020.

The birth rate is the number of births in a given year divided by the total mid-year population in that year. It is also known as crude birth rate. China's annual birth rate decreased from 18.2 per thousand people to 8.51 per thousand people while India's birth rate decreased from 36.2 per thousand people to 17.6 per thousand people. While China's birth rate per thousand decreased 53.2%, India's birth rate per thousand decreased 51.4% over the 40 years. Between 1980 and 2020, India's birth rate per thousand was always higher than those of China.

The natural increase rate is the difference between the crude birth rate and the crude death rate within a year. The natural increase rate in both nations decreased between 1980 and 2020. While China's natural increase rate decreased from 11.87 per thousand people to 1.45 per thousand people, India's natural increase rate decreased from 23.4 per thousand to 9.9 per thousand. While China's natural increase rate fell by 87.8%, India's natural increase rate declined 57.7%. China's natural increase rate decreased more than that of India.

Urbanization indicates the percentage of people living in urban places. From 1980 to 2019 (data for 2020 are not available), China's urban population increased from 20% to 62.7% while India's urban population climbed from 23.1% to 34.5%. China's percentage of the urban population increased about 213.5%, and India's percentage increased about 49.4% within 39 years. The percentage of China's urban population increased more than four times that of India.

With population change, economic development also changed in China and India. Between 1980 and 2020, China's total GDP increased from about $303 billion to about $14,860 billion, a 48-fold increase. During the same period, India's total GDP increased from about $189 billion to about $2,590 billion, an increase of 12.7 times. China's total GDP increased about four times that of India's within 40 years.

During the same period, China's per capita GDP increased from about $307 to about $10,580, a 33.5-fold increase. Different from the economic changes in China,

India's per capita GDP grew from about $271 to about $1,880, a 5.9-fold increase. Similar to the total GDP increase, China's per capita GDP increased about 5.7 times that of India within 40 years.

Obviously, India's total population expanded more rapidly than China's although its total fertility decreased more rapidly than China's between 1980 and 2020. Both China and India had a similar decrease in birth rate; however, China's natural increase rate fell much more rapidly than India's. At the same time, China's percentage of urban population increased more than four times that of India.

As a result of the population changes and changes in other factors, China's total GDP increased about four times India's. At the same time, China's per capita GDP increased about 5.7 times India's between 1980 and 2020. This meant that not only did China's total GDP increased more rapidly than India's, but individual Chinese also benefited more than individual Indians because of their much-reduced population growth.

There are many factors that may have contributed to these population differences. Changes in China and India may have contributed differently to economic development. Similarly, differences in economic development in the two societies affected population growth in the two societies. Therefore, population change and economic development may be correlated to each other in China and India.

Research Methods

Therefore, this chapter studies the relationship between population change and economic development in China and India empirically. Although population data are available between 1950 and 2020, the economic data available to the author were only between 1980 and 2020. Since the most dramatic population and economic changes occurred since 1980, the lack of comparable economic data between 1950 and 1979 should not affect the research fundamentally.

The Chinese population data were collected by the National Bureau of Statistics of China in 2021 (see Table 2.1). The Indian population data were collected by Macrotrends, the premier research platform for long-term investors, in 2021 (see Table 3.1). These population data include total population, annual TFR, birth rate, natural increase rate, and urbanization percentage for both China and India between 1950 and 2020. The economic data, including the total GDP and per capita GDP at 2020 US dollar prices, were estimated by the International Monetary Fund in 2021 (Table 5.1).

I used SPSS software to analyze Pearson correlations between total population, TFR, birth rate, annual natural increase rate, urbanization, total GDP, and per capita GDP in China and India. Then, I used Microsoft Word line charts to visually demonstrate the correlations between the total fertility, birth, and natural increase rates, urbanization, and per capita GDP in China and India. Since the correlations between the population variables and total GDP and per capita GDP are quite similar, I excluded them from figure demonstrations. The charts clearly show

Table 5.1 Economic Growth Rate in China and India (1980–2020)

Year	*Annual Growth Rate China*	*Annual Growth Rate India*	*Total GDP at 2020 Prices (Billions of US Dollars) China*	*Total GDP at 2020 Prices (Billions of US Dollars India*	*Per Capita GDP at 2020 Prices in US Dollars China*	*Per Capita GDP at 2020 Prices in US Dollars India*
1980	7.9	5.3	303.03	189.44	307.00	271.03
1981	5.1	6.0	288.73	196.54	288.53	274.73
1982	9.0	3.5	284.61	203.54	279.98	277.96
1983	10.8	7.3	305.43	222.05	296.51	296.29
1984	15.2	3.8	314.22	215.56	301.11	281.10
1985	13.5	5.3	310.15	237.62	293.01	302.95
1986	8.9	4.8	300.92	252.75	279.91	315.16
1987	11.7	4.0	327.72	283.75	299.83	346.17
1988	11.2	9.6	408.65	299.65	368.07	357.80
1989	4.2	5.9	458.17	301.23	406.52	352.18
1990	3.9	5.5	396.58	326.61	346.86	374.00
1991	9.3	1.1	413.22	274.84	356.77	308.37
1992	14.2	5.5	492.16	293.26	420.03	322.51
1993	13.9	4.8	617.43	284.19	520.96	306.44
1994	13.0	6.7	561.69	333.01	468.66	352.17
1995	10.9	7.6	731.02	366.60	603.54	380.32
1996	9.9	7.5	860.48	399.79	703.07	406.97
1997	9.2	4.0	957.99	423.19	774.91	422.81
1998	7.8	6.2	1020.00	428.77	820.91	420.57
1999	7.7	8.5	1090.00	466.84	865.23	449.73
2000	8.5	4.0	1210.00	476.64	951.15	451.11
2001	8.4	4.9	1330.00	493.93	1040.00	459.47
2002	9.1	3.9	1470.00	523.77	1140.00	479.06
2003	10.0	7.9	1660.00	618.37	1280.00	556.33
2004	10.2	7.8	1950.00	721.59	1500.00	638.79
2005	11.4	9.3	2290.00	834.22	1750.00	726.92
2006	12.7	9.3	2750.00	949.12	2100.00	814.35
2007	14.3	9.8	3560.00	1240.00	2690.00	1050.00
2008	9.7	3.9	4580.00	1220.00	3450.00	1020.00
2009	9.4	8.5	5090.00	1370.00	3810.00	1120.00
2010	10.6	10.3	6030.00	1710.00	4500.00	1380.00
2011	9.5	6.6	7490.00	1820.00	5560.00	1460.00
2012	7.9	5.5	8540.00	1830.00	6310.00	1440.00
2013	7.8	6.4	9630.00	1860.00	7070.00	1450.00
2014	7.3	7.4	10520.00	2040.00	7690.00	1570.00
2015	6.9	8.0	11110.00	2100.00	8080.00	1610.00
2016	6.8	8.3	11230.00	2290.00	8120.00	1730.00
2017	6.9	7.0	12270.00	2650.00	8820.00	1980.00
2018	6.7	6.1	13840.00	2710.00	9920.00	2010.00
2019	6.1	4.2	14400.00	2870.00	10290.00	2100.00
2020	1.9	−10.3	14860.00	2590.00	10580.00	1880.00

Source: Data Source: International Monetary Fund (2021). Data Mapper, Real GDP Growth: Annual Percentage Change, 1980–2025. Retrieved on March 26, 2021, from www.imf.org/external/datamapper/NGDP_RPCH@WEO/OEMDC/ADVEC/WEOWORLD/CHN

the correlations between population variables and per capita GDP and the developmental trends of population change and economic development in China and India simultaneously.

Correlations Between Population Change and Total GDP and Per Capita GDP in China and India

Table 5.2 lists all the correlations between total population growth, total fertility, birth rate, natural increase rate, urbanization percentage, total GDP, and per capita GDP in China. The growth of the total population was positively and strongly correlated to total GDP (.783) and per capita GDP (.786). The TFR was negatively and moderately correlated to total GDP (−.480) and per capita GDP (−.484). The birth rate was negatively and strongly correlated to total GDP (−.689) and per capita GDP (−.692). Similarly, the natural increase rate was negatively and strongly correlated to total GDP (−.721) and per capita GDP (−.724). Finally, urbanization was positive and strongly correlated to total GDP (.927) and per capita GDP (.930). All these correlations are indicated by two stars (**) which indicate that the correlation is statistically significant at the 0.01 level.

Table 5.3 lists all the correlations between total population growth, total fertility, birth rate, natural increase rate, urbanization percentage, total GDP, and per capita GDP in India. The growth of the total population was positively and strongly correlated to total GDP (.897) and per capita GDP (.898). The TFR was negatively and strongly correlated to total GDP (−.880) and per capita GDP (−.881). The birth rate was negatively and strongly correlated to total GDP (−.903) and per capita GDP (−.903). Similarly, the natural increase rate was negatively and strongly correlated to total GDP (−.936) and per capita GDP (−.936). Finally, urbanization was positive and strongly correlated to total GDP (.946) and per capita GDP (.945). All these correlations are statistically significant at the 0.01 level.

Figure 5.1 clearly demonstrates not only the positive correlation between population growth and per capita GDP but also the similar developmental trend of population and economic development in China and India. While China's population increased more slowly than India's population, China's per capita GDP increased much more rapidly than India's between 1980 and 2020. Nevertheless, the relationship between population growth and per capita GDP increased in China and India showed the same trend: When population growth leveled off, per capita GDP increased more rapidly.

Contrary to the positive correlation between the population and per capita GDP, the fertility rate was negatively related to per capita GDP in China and India. When the fertility rate decreased, per capita GDP increased in China and India.

Figure 5.2 demonstrates the correlation between the fertility rate and per capita GDP in China and India. When the fertility rate decreased in China and India, it decreased more in China than in India. Corresponding to the fertility decrease, per capita GDP increased in both China and India. Between 1980 and 2020, China's fertility decreased more rapidly, and its per capita GDP grew much more rapidly than India's.

Table 5.2 Correlations Between Population Variables and Economic Development in China

		China Population	*China Total Fertility*	*China Birth Rate*	*China Natural Increase Rate*	*China Urbanization*	*China Total GDP*	*China Per Capita GDP*
China Population	Pearson correlation	–						
	N	41						
China Total Fertility	Pearson correlation	−.891**	–					
	Sig. (two-tailed)	<.001						
	N	41	41					
China Birth Rate	Pearson correlation	−.910**	.874**	–				
	Sig. (two-tailed)	<.001	<.001					
	N	41	41	41				
China Natural Increase Rate	Pearson correlation	−.917**	.865**	.997**	–			
	Sig. (two-tailed)	<.001	<.001	<.001				
	N	41	41	41	41			
China Urbanization	Pearson correlation	.946**	−.727**	−.872**	−.893**	–		
	Sig. (two-tailed)	<.001	<.001	<.001	<.001			
	N	41	41	41	41	41		
China Total GDP	Pearson correlation	.783**	−.480**	−.689**	−.721**	.927**	–	
	Sig. (two-tailed)	<.001	.002	<.001	<.001	<.001		
	N	41	41	41	41	41	41	
China Per Capita GDP	Pearson correlation	.786**	−.484**	−.692**	−.724**	.930**	1.000**	–
	Sig. (2-tailed)	<.001	.001	<.001	<.001	<.001	<.001	
	N	41	41	41	41	41	41	41

Notes: **Correlation is statistically significant at the 0.01 level (two-tailed).

Table 5.3 Correlations Between Population Variables and Economic Development in India

		India Population	*India Total Fertility*	*India Birth Rate*	*India Natural Increase Rate*	*India Urbanization*	*India Total GDP*	*India Per Capita GDP*
India population	Pearson correlation	–						
	N	41						
India total fertility	Pearson correlation	−.999**	–					
	Sig. (two-tailed)	<.001						
	N	41	41					
India birth rate	Pearson correlation	−.999**	.998**	–				
	Sig. (two-tailed)	<.001	<.001					
	N	41	41	41				
India Natural increase rate	Pearson correlation	−.993**	.989**	.996**	–			
	Sig. (two-tailed)	<.001	<.001	<.001				
	N	41	41	41	41			
India urbanization	Pearson correlation	.989**	−.983**	−.990**	−.997**	–		
	Sig. (two-tailed)	<.001	<.001	<.001	<.001			
	N	40	40	40	40	40		
India total GDP	Pearson correlation	.897**	−.880**	−.903**	−.936**	.946**	–	
	Sig. (two-tailed)	<.001	<.001	<.001	<.001	<.001		
	N	41	41	41	41	40	41	
India per capita GDP	Pearson correlation	.898**	−.881**	−.903**	−.936**	.945**	.999**	–
	Sig. (two-tailed)	<.001	<.001	<.001	<.001	<.001	<.001	
	N	41	41	41	41	40	41	41

Notes: **Correlation is significant at the 0.01 level (two-tailed).

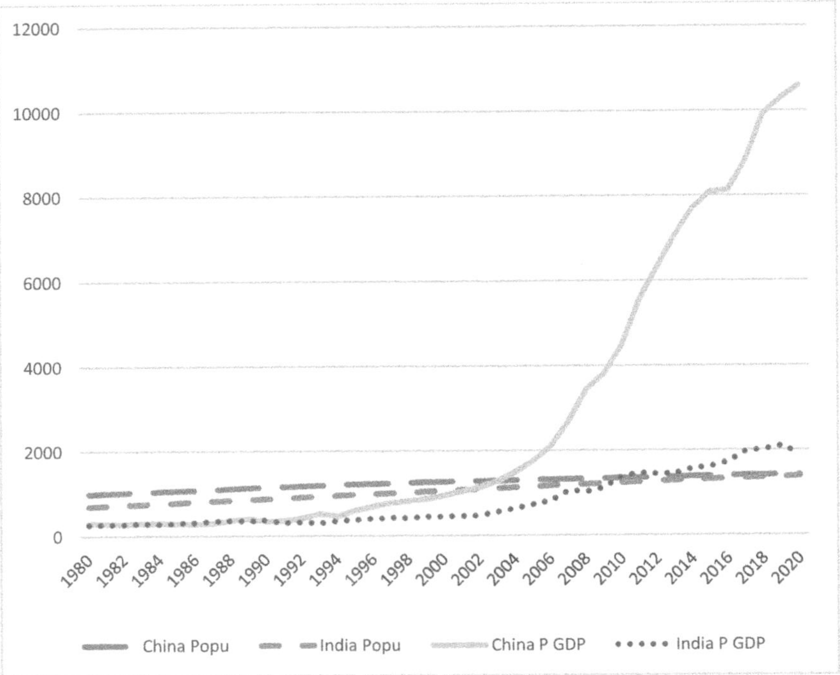

Figure 5.1 Population (in Millions) and Per Capita GDP (in US Dollars) in China and India

Sources:

1. China's population data are according to National Bureau of Statistics of China. 2021. National Data, Population. Retrieved on September 21, 2022, at http://www.stats.gov.cn/tjsj/ndsj/2021/indexch.htm.
2. Indian population data are collected by the Macrotrends which compiled the data according to the information provided by the United Nations. The data are retrieved on April 1, 2021, from https://www.macrotrends.net/countries/IND/india/fertility-rate.
3. GDP data source: International Monetary Fund. 2021. Data Mapper, Real GDP Growth: Annual Percentage Change, 1980–2025. Retrieved on March 26, 2021, from https://www.imf.org/external/datamapper/NGDP_RPCH@WEO/OEMDC/ADVEC/WEOWORLD/CHN.

Figure 5.3 clearly demonstrates the correlations between birth rate and per capita GDP in China and India. The correlation between birth rate and per capita GDP indicates the same developmental trend. When the birth rate decreased, per capita GDP increased. When China's birth rate declined more than India's, China's per capita GDP rose more than India's.

.Figure 5.4 demonstrates the correlation between natural increase rate and per capita GDP in China and India. The natural increase rate of population was negatively and strongly correlated with per capita GDP in the two countries. When the natural increase rate decreased, per capita GDP increased in both societies, but it increased much more rapidly in China for the 40 years.

Figure 5.5 demonstrates the correlations between urbanization and per capita GDP in China and India. The increase in the urban population percentage in China

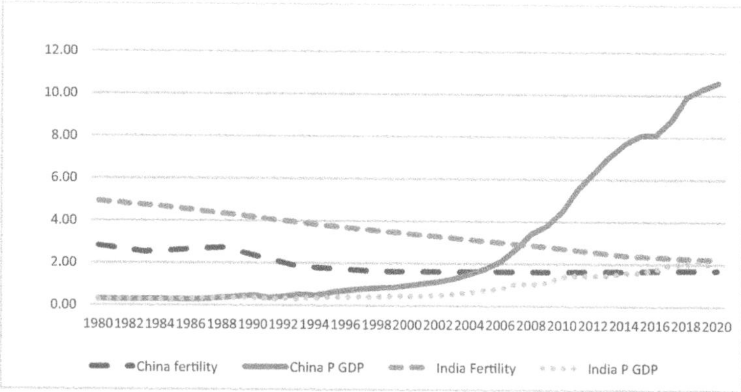

Figure 5.2 Total Fertility and Per Capita GDP ($1,000) in China and India

Sources:

1. China's population data are according to National Bureau of Statistics of China. 2021. National Data, Population. Retrieved on September 21, 2022, at http://www.stats.gov.cn/tjsj/ndsj/2021/indexch.htm.
2. Indian population data are collected by the Macrotrends which compiled the data according to the information provided by the United Nations. The data are retrieved on April 1, 2021, from https://www.macrotrends.net/countries/IND/india/fertility-rate.
3. GDP data source: International Monetary Fund. 2021. Data Mapper, Real GDP Growth: Annual Percentage Change, 1980–2025. Retrieved on March 26, 2021, from https://www.imf.org/external/datamapper/NGDP_RPCH@WEO/OEMDC/ADVEC/WEOWORLD/CHN.

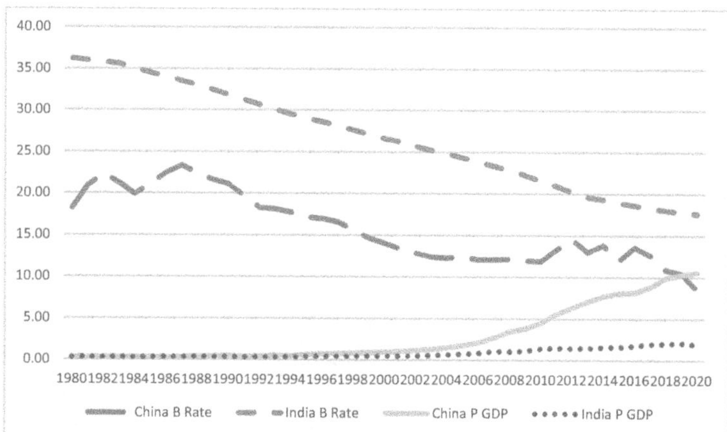

Figure 5.3 Population Birth Rate and Per Capita GDP ($1,000) in China and India

Sources:

1. China's population data are according to National Bureau of Statistics of China. 2021. National Data, Population. Retrieved on September 21, 2022, at http://www.stats.gov.cn/tjsj/ndsj/2021/indexch.htm.
2. Indian population data are collected by the Macrotrends which compiled the data according to the information provided by the United Nations. The data are retrieved on April 1, 2021, from https://www.macrotrends.net/countries/IND/india/fertility-rate.
3. GDP data source: International Monetary Fund. 2021. Data Mapper, Real GDP Growth: Annual Percentage Change, 1980–2025. Retrieved on March 26, 2021, from https://www.imf.org/external/datamapper/NGDP_RPCH@WEO/OEMDC/ADVEC/WEOWORLD/CHN.

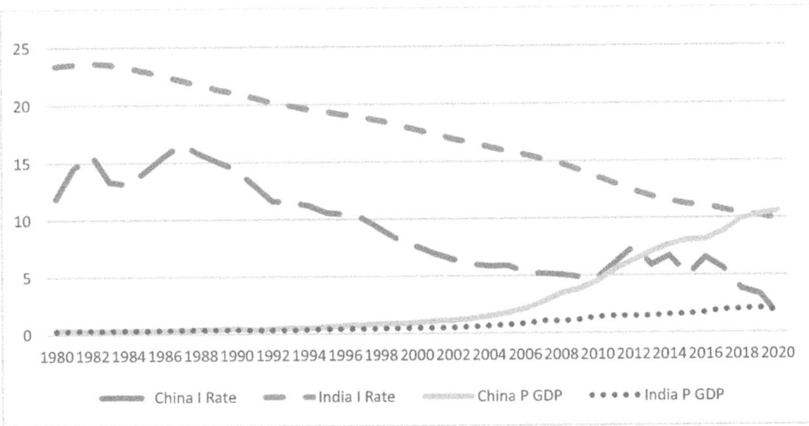

Figure 5.4 Population Increase Rate and Per Capita GDP ($1,000) in China and India

Sources:

1. China's population data are according to National Bureau of Statistics of China. 2021. National Data, Population. Retrieved on September 21, 2022, at http://www.stats.gov.cn/tjsj/ndsj/2021/indexch.htm.
2. Indian population data are collected by the Macrotrends which compiled the data according to the information provided by the United Nations. The data are retrieved on April 1, 2021, from https://www.macrotrends.net/countries/IND/india/fertility-rate.
3. GDP data source: International Monetary Fund. 2021. Data Mapper, Real GDP Growth: Annual Percentage Change, 1980–2025. Retrieved on March 26, 2021, from https://www.imf.org/external/datamapper/NGDP_RPCH@WEO/OEMDC/ADVEC/WEOWORLD/CHN

and India was positively and strongly correlated to per capita GDP in the two societies. When the percentage of urban population increased, per capita GDP increased. Both urbanization and per capita GDP increased, but growth was much more rapid in China than in India between 1980 and 2020.

All the information indicates that population change, including changes in fertility, birth rate, natural increase rate, and urbanization, was strongly related to the economic development in China and India. While population increases, economy develops, or while economy develops, population increases. Similarly, urbanization was positively and strongly related to the increase in total GDP and per capita GDP. As the percentage of the urban population increased, the economy developed more rapidly, or as the economy developed more rapidly, the percentage of the urban population increased more rapidly.

On the other hand, total fertility, birth, and natural increase rates were negatively related to both total GDP and per capita GDP. While total fertility, birth rate, and natural increase rate fell, economic development increased, or, conversely, while economic growth increased, fertility, birth, and natural increase rates declined. It is possible that the decrease in fertility, birth, and natural increase rates enabled the economy to develop more rapidly, or when the economy developed more rapidly, it caused a decrease in the total fertility, birth, and natural increase rates in China and India.

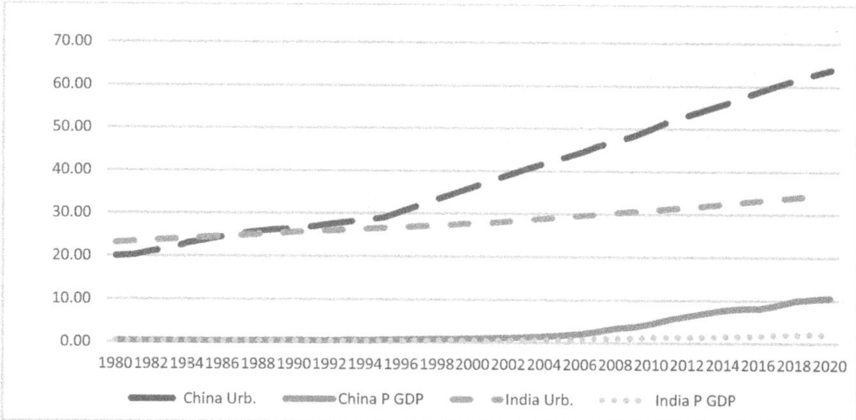

Figure 5.5 Urbanization and Per Capita GDP ($1,000) in China and India

Sources:

1. China's population data are according to National Bureau of Statistics of China. 2021. National Data, Population. Retrieved on September 21, 2022, at http://www.stats.gov.cn/tjsj/ndsj/2021/indexch.htm.
2. Indian population data are collected by the Macrotrends which compiled the data according to the information provided by the United Nations. The data are retrieved on April 1, 2021, from https://www.macrotrends.net/countries/IND/india/fertility-rate.
3. GDP data source: International Monetary Fund. 2021. Data Mapper, Real GDP Growth: Annual Percentage Change, 1980–2025. Retrieved on March 26, 2021, from https://www.imf.org/external/datamapper/NGDP_RPCH@WEO/OEMDC/ADVEC/WEOWORLD/CHN.

Conclusions and Discussions

The empirical data analyses have indicated that population growth and urbanization are positively related to economic development, but total fertility, birth, and natural increase rates are negatively related to economic development in both countries. When population increase slowed down, their economies developed more rapidly. Population growth, either because it increased demand, stimulated investment, or consumed more products, accompanied economic growth. Economic development may better support population growth; however, in a modern society in which food is no longer a major problem, it is unlikely to promote population growth.

At the same time, rapid population growth may consume a large portion of economic development and reduce investment. Urbanization can follow from economic development. On the other hand, when more people move into urban areas, limited space and a more competitive social environment dampen the demand for more children because raising children in urban areas costs much more than in rural areas. Urban life is less likely to support having many children for most people.

On the other hand, decreases in total fertility, birth, and natural increase rates were all negatively related to economic development. When those rates decrease more rapidly, the economy develops more rapidly, and per capita income is more likely to increase. With decreases in fertility, birth, and natural increase rates, women are more likely to work outside of the house with their participation enhancing economic development. The community or the government may be more likely to invest in infrastructure and industry rather than providing the basic needs of society, such as food, water, and schools.

Having compared economic growth and population transitions in China and India between 1990 and 2018, Chaurasia (2021) found that, in China, most economic growth has contributed to the improvement of living standards, but a substantial proportion of economic growth in India has been the result of demographic factors that contributed little to the improvement of the quality of life for the Indians. The major difference between the two nations is that China has reached an advanced stage of population transition while India is still stuck in the middle of the population transition path.

This chapter provides some support to Chaurasia's conclusions. Population increase, urbanization, the decline in fertility, birth, and natural increase rates all indicate a similar pattern of population change and economic development. All the figures provided in this chapter demonstrate a similar population and economic development trend or population transition. China's more rapid population transition, which has been considerably promoted by its effective population control, has enabled China to develop its economy more rapidly than India. Yet India's economic development may accelerate in the future when its total fertility, birth, and natural increase rates further decline or when its population transition catches up with China's.

Based on the correlation between population change and economic development in China and India, it is reasonable to assume that population growth will simultaneously bring about economic development. However, it is the rapid decrease in fertility, birth, and natural increase rates accompanied by a rapid urbanization that promotes rapid economic development. On the other hand, rapid economic development also enhances urbanization and is conducive to a decrease in fertility, birth, and natural increase rates. Of course, population change and economic development in China and India are also affected by other factors, such as economic policy, social structure, women's status, education, and government efficiency, in addition to population control policies.

References

Birdsall, Nancy. 1977. "Analytical Approaches to the Relationship of Population Growth and Development". *Population and Development Review* 3: 63–102.

Birdsall, Nancy, Allen C. Kelly, James B. Duck and Steven Sinding. 2001. *Population Matters: Demography, Growth, and Poverty in the Developing World*. Oxford: Oxford University Press.

Birdsall, Nancy and S. W. Sinding. 2001. *Population Matters – Demographic Change, Economic Growth, and Poverty in the Developing World*. Oxford: Oxford University Press.

Bloom, D. E., D. Canning and J. Sevilla. 2003. *The Demographic Dividend: A New Perspective on the Economic Consequences of Population Change*. Santa Monica: RAND.

Bloom, D. E. and J. G. Williamson. 1998. "Demographic Transition and Economic Miracles in Emerging Asia". *World Bank Economic Review* 12: 419–455.

Chaurasia, Aalok Ranjan. 2021. "Economic Growth and Population Transition in China and India 1990–2018". *China Population and Development Studies* 4: 229–261.

Fox, Sean and Tim Dyson. 2015. "Is Population Growth Good or Bad for Economic Development?" *International Growth Center*. Retrieved on April 5, 2021 from theigc.org.

Galor, O. and D. Weil. 2000. "Population, Technology, and Growth: From Malthus Stagnation to the Demographic Transition and Beyond". *American Economic Review* 90: 806–828.

Headey, Derek and Andrew Hodge. 2009. "The Effects of Population Growth on Economic Growth: A Meta-regression Analysis of the Macroeconomic Literature". *Population and Development Review* 35 (2): 1–28.

Huang, Tai-Hsin and Zixiong Xie. 2013. "Population and Economic Growth: A Simultaneous Equation Perspective". *Applied Economics* 45: 3820–3826.

International Monetary Fund. 2021. "Data Mapper, Real GDP Growth: Annual Percentage Change, 1980–2025". Retrieved on March 26, 2021 from www.imf.org/external/datamapper/NGDP_RPCH@WEO/OEMDC/ADVEC/WEOWORLD/CHN.

Kelly, A. 2001. "The Population Debate in Historical Perspective: Revisionism Revised", in Birdsall, Kelly, and Sinding (eds) *Population Matters: Demography, Growth, and Poverty in the Developing World*. New York, NY: Oxford University Press,24–54.

Kremer, M. 1993. "Population Growth and Technological Change: One Million B. C. to 1990". *The Quarterly Journal of Economics* 108: 681–716.

Kumar, Mahendra. 2021. "Population Growth and Economic Development: A Close Review". Retrieved on April 3, 2021 from www.economicsdiscussion.net/economic-development/population-growth-and-economic-development-a-close-view/11808.

Kuznets, Simon S. 1966. *Modern Economic Growth: Rate, Structure and Spread*. New Haven, CT: Yale University Press.

Kuznets, Simon S. 1973. *Population Capital and Growth: Selected Essays*. New York, NY: W. W. Norton and Company.

Li, H. and J. Zhang. 2007. "Do High Birth Rates Hamper Economic Growth?" *Review of Economics and Statistics* 89: 110–117.

Mason, A. (ed.). 2001. *Population Change and Economic Development*. Stanford, CA: Stanford University Press.

McNicoll, Geoffrey. 1984. "Consequences of Rapid Population Growth: An Overview and Assessment". *Population and Development Review* 10: 177–240.

McNicoll, Geoffrey. 2006. "Policy Lessons of the East Asian Demographic Transition". *Population and Development Review* 32(1): 1–25.

Simon, Julian. L. 1977. *The Economics of Population Growth*. Princeton, NJ: Princeton University Press.

Simon, L. 1981. *The Ultimate Resource*. Princeton, NJ: Princeton University Press.

Yamaguchi, M. 1973. *Technical Change and Population Growth in the Economic Development of Japan* (Economic Development Center Annual Report). Minneapolis, MN: University of Minnesota.

Yao, Wanjun, Tomoko Kinugasa and Shigeyuki Hamori. 2013. "An Empirical Analysis of the Relationship Between Economic Development and Population Growth in China". *Applied Economics* 45(33): 4651–4661.

6 Social and Cultural Differences Between China and India

Introduction

Since the establishment of their new governments in the late 1940s, both China and India perceived their huge and rapidly increasing populations as obstacles to their socioeconomic development, and both adopted population control policies to curb their population growth. While the Indian government adopted and implemented population control policies in 1952, it took the Chinese government until the 1960s. Their similar efforts, however, yielded different results, and their populations have experienced different changes during the past seven decades. While China's population has grown 3.4% less than the world's population, India's population has grown 3% faster (Wang, 2018). According to the United Nations' Department of Economic and Social Affairs, China and India will each have about 1.4 billion people when the world's population reaches 8.0 billion in November 2022. India is projected to surpass China to become the most populous country in the world in 2023 (United Nations Department of Economic and Social Affairs, 2022).

While these two countries' population controls have led to different population trajectories, many wonder what has caused the differences. Some scholars have done excellent work comparing population control policies (Liu and Liu, 2010; Stolc, 2008), others compared demographic transitions, urbanization, or economic development (Choudhry and Elhorst, 2010; Jones and Visaria, 1998; Golley and Tyers, 2013; Livi-Bacci, 2012, and still others have compared future populations, or consequences of the population controls in China and India (Eggleston, 2016).

These comparisons of population control policies or policy implementations, however, mostly focus on demographic factors, such as birth rate, death rate, gender structure, or natural increase rate. Some scholars may cite social or cultural factors to explain the differences, but the social and cultural factors are normally not the focus of their research. As a result, most of these comparisons are limited in understanding how the population control policies and the population changes are so different between China and India.

Both China and India are great civilizations with unique histories and cultures that have had fundamental effects on their socioeconomic developments, including government policies and population changes. This chapter compares those social and cultural factors, including religion and traditional values related to population,

DOI: 10.4324/9781003307419-6

ethnicity and languages, social class, social structure, the family, the social status and education of women, and the functional differences between the governments. These factors affect not only population control policy, policy implementations, and population changes but also the functioning of the world's two most populous societies.

Behind these factors are two fundamental differences between China and India. First, Chinese and Indian societies have developed differently. China has had different states with different languages, different cultures, different political ideologies, and different government structures before Qin Shi Huang unified China in 221 BCE. However, after Qin Shi Huang unified China and established the Qin Dynasty, its feudal system ended, and he established a strong central government. Shi Huang, the first emperor of China, unified the Chinese languages and its system of weights and measures. He centralized judicial, executive, and military power in the central government, divided Chinese territory into 36 *Jun* (prefectures), and built highways to connect them all. Similarly, people's values and behavior norms were also unified.

Although the Qin Dynasty was short-lived, the sophisticated bureaucratic government system it established lasted for more than 2,000 years. During the following Han Dynasty between 202 BCE and 220 CE, the Chinese improved the government bureaucracy. Those serving in the bureaucratic system gained their positions through nationwide government examinations. The Han Dynasty promoted Confucianism throughout the nation and further unified people's behaviors. Since then, Chinese society has become and mostly remained a unified society with its large population under the control of a strong central government.

Although China fell into chaos and suffered from Japan's invasion after the 1911 fall of the Qing Dynasty (the last dynasty), in 1949, the newly established Communist government led by Mao Zedong quickly put mainland China back in order and regained tight control of Chinese society. Starting in the 1950s, the establishment of People's Communes in rural areas and the nationalization of corporations and financial institutes—aided by the popularization of Mandarin—consolidated central government control over the world's most populous nation.

In contrast, there was no Qin Shi Huang in India. Although Chandragupta Maurya unified a large part of the Indian subcontinent and established the Maurya Dynasty about the same time as Qin Shi Huang unified China, Chandragupta Maurya's consolidation never achieved the same depth or breadth. Even when the Maurya kingdom expanded to become an empire that reached its peak under Ashoka, it was a loosely knit empire. For example, the feudal system continued with kingdoms or tribes ruling different parts of the subcontinent, and different religions and languages continued to develop. Indian society was never unified and always difficult to change. Many small kingdoms came and went. Often a new ruler would capture the symbolic seat of power and rule on as those before him had done. The divided Indian subcontinent could be defeated easily, but society itself remained almost unconquered and unchanged.

The state as a sovereign agency with powers to change society, alter its economic relations, control its beliefs, or rewrite its laws did not exist in India (Khilnani,

1997). Therefore, the Indian subcontinent had never been totally or actually unified by a central government before the British colonized the region. Khilnani commented as follows:

> Inhabitants of the land called India had been of interest only to outsiders: to the Greeks, who first name the land Indica, to travelers, traders and invaders, and then most comprehensively to the British, who in their train-spotting way darted across the subcontinent mapping, tabulating and classifying the territory and people that gradually came into their possession . . . It was the British interest in determining geographical boundaries that by an Act of Parliament in 1899 converted "India" from the name of a cultural region into a precise, pink territory.
>
> (Khilnani, 1997: 155)

Accordingly, Embree has pointed out that India lacked the elements generally regarded as the essential ingredients of nationality, such as a common language, common religious tradition, and limited experience shared by the majority of the people. Embree adds that even in 1880, India had no physical, political, social, religious, or linguistic unity (1972).

Even after the British government formally controlled the subcontinent for about a century, there were still more than 560 princely states in India when the subcontinent obtained its independence in 1947 (Guha, 2007). After a central government had been established and Pakistan became a different nation, an independent Indian society still remained separated by different languages, races, religions, and castes.

Therefore, in their long histories, unification is a more common phenomenon in China and division is more common in India. According to Professor San at Beijing University, China was under the control of a unified central government headed by an emperor and his family during 70% of its history. Contrary to China, during 70% of its history, India was divided and under the control of many different governments or kings (San, 2007). Obviously, Chinese and Indian societies, situated on different sides of the Himalayan range, are structured differently. This is a fundamental difference between China and India. Without an adequate understanding of it, the differences between the two largest countries appear arbitrary.

Because of its unique history, plus the mild non-cooperative movement, which led to the independence of India, the newly established government of the Republic of India was unable to implement fundamental changes. First-generation leaders, such as Nehru, though, wanted to carry out a thorough land reform and more radical changes to traditional Indian society. In contrast to India, the Chinese revolution had gone through many years of bloody fighting. When the People's Republic of China was formed in 1949, the new government regained total control of Chinese society. As a result, the new Chinese government could carry out thorough land reforms in rural areas and revolutionize industry and business in urban areas. At the same time, the new government could right away rid itself of traditional social ills such as prostitution, bandits, opium, and polygamy. This difference also gave the new Chinese and Indian governments different powers to adopt and implement policies in the days to come.

Second, the Indian society has been much more fundamentally affected than Chinese society by people from other parts of the world. Ever since Indian civilization started, its favorable geographic conditions and great development of agriculture attracted people from the North and other parts of the world. Repeatedly, people mostly from the North kept on coming or invading the Indian subcontinent. For example, the Aryans, the Greeks, the Turks, the Afghans, the Mughals, and the British all came and brought their religions, languages, and cultures along with them to India. Those foreigners just kept coming, conquering native Indians, and adding new cultures to Indian civilization. "Several centuries-old flows of outsiders and continuous merger of culture with different racial and religious groups into Indian subcontinent over the period of time have heavily influenced India's culture and society" (Khemundu, 2019: 473). The differences between European countries were much smaller than the differences between the states of India. More specifically, the diversities of race, language, and religion in India were far greater than the diversities between European countries (Strachey, 1988).

Contrary to India, China has been influenced much less by invaders or people from other parts of the world. Before the 19th century, China was also highly developed in agriculture. Similar to India, China was invaded repeatedly by people from the North. Although China's geographic conditions were more open to invasion than India's, the Chinese kept on fighting back and repelled most of their northerly invaders. For example, under a strong central government, the Chinese built the famous Great Wall which extended for thousands of miles to keep most invaders out. Had India wanted to build a wall to keep invaders out, it would be much easier for them, for the narrowest point of the Khyber Pass through which the invaders normally came is only about 600 meters wide (Liu, 2019).

During its long history, Mongolians and Mandarins from the North succeeded in invading Han-controlled China. Mongolians established the Yuan Dynasty and forced a caste system on the Chinese population. However, Mongolian rule was overthrown by the Han Chinese within a century, and the caste system was discarded. The Mandarins established the Qing Dynasty, which lasted for more than two centuries, but it was also overthrown by the Han Chinese in 1911.

Although Mongolians and the Mandarins ruled China for a total of 364 years, they mostly adopted Chinese culture instead of forcing their cultures onto the enormous Chinese Han population. During the 19th and 20th centuries, China was invaded by Western nations, and the Chinese always fought back severely. As a result, China has never been totally occupied or colonized by any Western nations. During its long history, the most fundamental and lasting external influence on Chinese culture has been Buddhism, which originated in India. Many Chinese government officials or scholars felt that Buddhism could be supplementary to Chinese culture (Tan, 2007). Similarly, many Chinese started to learn from Western societies when they realized that China had fallen behind the Western nations, especially in science and technology. Although Western nations have influenced China since the middle of the 19th century, their influence on China was much smaller than and different from their influence on India.

When India obtained its independence in 1947, the new government mostly inherited the British political system. It also relied on members of the Indian Civil Service (ICS) that used to serve the British colonial government to run the government for the new Indian state. Although the ICS was replaced by the Indian Administrative Service (IAS) in 1950, the IAS continued the work laid down by the ICS, such as running elections (Guha, 2007). Contrary to India, when the Chinese Communist Party established the new government in 1949, they eradicated almost everything established by the previous Nationalist government. When the Japanese invaders were driven out of China in 1945, everything established by the Japanese invaders was destroyed. At the same time, almost all Western establishments fled China after 1949. As a result, while India's nationalist government inherited much from the colonial government, the CCP established a new Chinese state.

After the establishment of the PRC in 1949, external influence was substantially reduced in the 1950s except from the former Soviet Union, which was mostly reduced in the 1960s. Although Western influence on China has increased substantially since the 1980s, influence has been filtered by the Chinese government. In contrast to China, the influence from Western countries was strong before the establishment of the Republic of India in 1947, and it has remained strong ever since. Although strong religious traditions have prevented the spread of Western cultures in Indian society, the adoption of the British political system and the use of English as an official language have allowed substantial Western influence on Indian society. This fundamental difference between India and China has made the current cultures of China and India quite different, partly explaining why Western nations have treated China and India differently.

Chinese and Indian societies have developed different religions, values, ethnicities, languages, social classes, family structures, and different social statuses and forms of women's education. With all these differences, the Chinese and Indian governments have functioned differently when they attempted to control population growth. These differences have also determined the functioning of the two societies.

Religion and Traditional Differences

The most fundamental historical difference between India and China has been that Indian society is religious and Chinese society is mostly secular. This difference has fundamentally affected population control policies and population changes in China and India.

During the early part of Chinese history, most Chinese scholars paid great attention to the human relations in their society. On the other hand, most Indian scholars paid great attention to the relationships between God and people. Although both traditional Chinese and Indians would like to have a harmonious relationship with the natural environment, family was the center of people's life in China and religion was the center of people's life in India. While most Chinese paid attention to life in this world, Indians normally expected there to be a next life.

Accordingly, Indian morality was mostly developed from religious beliefs while Chinese morality was mostly developed from relations between different groups of people. As a result, India had developed many religions that dominate people's lives, with Hinduism being the dominant religion in traditional Indian society. Instead of religions, the Chinese developed different philosophies of life, with Confucianism dominant. Confucianism is not a religion; instead, it is an ethical guide to life, and according to Confucianism, a good moral character is most important to individuals.

Ever since his philosophy became the dominant ideology in China 2,000 years ago during the Han Dynasty, Confucius has been considered as the greatest teacher in China. He was respected highly because his teachings provided a standard for people's behaviors. However, those who respected Confucius or those who strove to spread Confucian ideology have never formed a religious organization, nor have they gone to Confucian Temples as Christians go to their churches every Sunday. The formal ceremonies to show respect to Confucius are usually held by government officials, and these ceremonies are political events rather than religious ceremonies.

According to Confucianism, each person in Chinese society should behave according to his/her status. For example, between the emperor and his officials, the emperor guided his officials. Between father and son, the father guided the son. Between husband and wife, the husband guided his wife. Expectations about individuals in social relationships required that each person had to be benevolent, wise, righteous, show propriety, and be trustworthy. Although Confucian rituals, order, and obedience have become internalized standards of behaviors for the Chinese people, Confucianism has never become a religion there.

For more than 2,000 years, China has never developed a dominant religion; people practice different religions. Confucius philosophy has had the strongest influence on the Chinese people. Nevertheless, Confucius has never become a God as Jesus and Brahma did, and Confucius never had his philosophy elevated to the status of a holy canon. At the same time, Confucius had no fundamental religious experience, no revelation; he achieved no inner rebirth, and he was not a mystic. In China's long history, many religions existed mostly side by side peacefully. At the same time, Chinese society has never been divided into a checkerboard pattern of religious states. The country has always been free from religious wars and strife that shaped much of the history of Europe and the Middle East.

Consequently, today's Chinese society is mostly a secular society. Although Buddhism (18.2%), Christianity (5.1%), Islam (1.8%), Hinduism (<0.1%), Judaism (<0.1%) (CIA, 2022a), and Daoism are widely distributed throughout the country, the majority of the Chinese have never been converted to any of these religions. None of the religions has ever become strong enough to make its values become government policy or strongly influence government policy. While Buddhism, Daoism, and Confucian philosophy have been practiced in China and influenced people's views of life for many centuries, Confucius' behavior guidance has had a dominant influence on Chinese society. In fact, Confucius was guided by the idea of an encompassing community and his passion was for beauty, order, truthfulness, and happiness in the world (Jaspers, 1957).

When talking about population, the Chinese have not inherited a strong religion that may have operated to prevent them from engaging in family planning or having abortions. Although, traditionally, Confucianism encouraged married couples to have more children, especially more sons, and the influence of this traditional value has substantially declined during the early and middle of the 20th century, when it was repeatedly criticized in Chinese society. For those who have strong religious beliefs or who evaluate a society through a strongly religious perspective, it may be difficult to understand the behavior of the Chinese people. In other words, people from Western or Indian societies have to cross their own religious boundaries or put their religious beliefs aside so that they can understand China.

In contrast to China, India is a highly religious society in which people practice all kinds of religions. After thousands of years of development, almost every individual in India is religious. Specifically, 79.8% of Indians are Hindus, 14.2% are Muslims, 2.3% are Christians, 1.7% are Sikhs, and 2% practice other unspecified religions (CIA, 2022b). Almost 100% of the population are religious.

Among different religions in India, Hinduism is the most commonly practiced religion and the Hindu canons make most people believe that the status quo is God's will. Everyone should accept his present condition as foreordained. If someone suffers, that person is destined to suffer. He or she should forbear and wait for a better life next time. Because of this strong religious belief, Indian society was highly stable and had a strong tendency to remain stagnant when people were born into different castes with highly proscribed roles from which one could not exit.

While Hinduism is dominant, Islam also has a strong and increasing influence on India's population. Within each religion in India, there are numerous branches, and each is different from the others. The Indian people live not only religiously but also differently. Unlike Christians, Muslims, or Jews, who believe in one god, Indians have their faith in numerous gods. In fact, no one actually knows how many gods are there in India. According to Vedas, there are 33 Gods. However, many Indians believe that there are 33 million Gods and Goddesses.

Therefore, it is difficult to identify a universal ideology except the caste system. The caste system originated from racial differences, and it does not weld society into obedience to a central power as in China. Instead, it is a decentralizing system, focusing loyalties at the caste level. General Indian philosophies and religious beliefs contain fundamental but diverse views, theories, and systems through which it is almost impossible to single out characteristics shared by all (Encyclopedia Britannica, 1978).

In India, religious beliefs are deeply embedded in people's minds, and people are supposed to or expected to follow their religions without doubt. There are a number of built-in traditional and religious checks on fertility: an emphasis on early marriage, preference for a son, and stigma related to infertility.

> Man and woman find their need for children repeated and reinforced in religion. Hindu Scripture teaches that a man remains in debt to his ancestors until

> he produces a son; that a son can save his father's soul from a terrible fate in the afterward, especially by performing the memorial rites called sraddh.
>
> (Mandelbaum, 1974: 21–22)

Owing to women's low status, a girl is expected to marry as early as possible and to have a son quickly to raise her social status (Srinivasan, 2017). In other words, there are no religious beliefs or teachings that support population control or abortion. At the same time, the differences in religion also make the Indians more spiritual, more philosophical, and more interested in discussion of issues while the Chinese are worldlier, more practical, and more likely to get things done.

Different Traditional Values Related to Population

China and India have largely shared traditional attitudes toward birth. Since patriarchal Chinese society worships ancestors and the patriarchal lineage system depends on sons to carry on family names, many Chinese thought that the more children one had the happier life would be and the earlier one had a son the sooner fortune would follow.

Similarly, most people in Indian society wanted to have at least two or three sons and a total of six children was a desirable number for many couples. To many Indians, especially farmers, children were their future and indispensable property. Therefore, the more sons one had, the more prosperous he would be. Couples who had a baby boy first were considered the luckiest. The roots of the patriarchal and patrilineal system of family life and inheritance can be traced back to the Vedic periods and form part of the collective consciousness of Hindu society. Such traditional views or values are persistent in today's Indian society.

In India,

> a son was necessary not only to continue the family line or *gotra* (clan or lineage) but also to liberate the departed souls of parents and grandparents by offering prayers and gifts every year on their death anniversaries. Life in this world and the other after death were considered incomplete and unfulfilled without a son. Those who had no son were permitted to adopt a daughter's child as their son after an appropriate religious ceremony. After adoption, the grandson would take over the religious duties of a son.
>
> (Srinivasan, 2017: 94).

Both China and India have strong traditions established by Confucianism in China or different religions in India; such traditions are conducive to population growth. However, closely related to religious or non-religious values in China and India, Ancient Chinese and Indian scholars had different perspectives on population. Although most of the ancient Chinese scholars believed that an increase in population was a symbol of prosperity, scholars, and political figures, such as Lao-tzu, Han Fei-tzu, Confucius, and Shang Yang, did not believe a large population was necessarily good.

For example, Lao-tzu believed that more people would cause a lack of commodities, and a peaceful life could only be obtained by having small states and a small population. Similarly, Han Fei-tzu believed that a smaller population would produce prosperity and stability. Confucius pointed out that population growth should be carried out to the amount of tillable land and that too many people would lower living standards. Shang Yang also believed that population and land should perfectly fit together. During the 18th and 19th centuries, scholars like Hong Liangji and Wang Shiduo repeatedly pointed out that overpopulation had caused serious socioeconomic problems, and they strongly advocated restrictive population controls (Wang, 1999).

Yet almost all scholars and religious leaders in India believed that population growth was good for society. For example, Kudiliya said that villages and towns should be large. Too few people have bad effects (Gao, 1985). Although those beliefs existed a long time ago, they still influence people's ideas today. In India, no religious beliefs encourage family planning, and none approve of abortion. The religions to which people subscribe share the idea that children are God-given, and to accept children is to accept a god's gift. These religious beliefs are almost unshakable in India, and Hinduism has been related to all aspects of life, including population.

The current fundamental difference in Chinese and Indian society is that in China, the tradition has been repeatedly criticized during the past century and its influences have been reduced in Chinese society while the tradition in India has remained little changed. The Chinese traditions have been criticized first by the May Fourth Movement of 1919, which attacked Confucian philosophy and traditional beliefs. Large-scale political movements from the 1950s through the 1970s further reduced the influence of Confucianism on Chinese society. Similarly, rituals that tend to maintain the old hierarchical systems in China have been severely criticized since the beginning of the 20th century. The influence of the Confucian principle of filial piety and fraternal duty, which attached great importance to the survival of the family name and indirectly contributed to population growth, has been substantially reduced. Since China's economic reforms started in the later 1970s, many Western values, such as individualism, have fundamentally affected Chinese society and further reduced Chinese responsibility to their families. Individualistic perspectives have reduced many individuals' willingness to have children or even get married.

In India, in contrast, religious traditions remain largely intact, and their influence continues to be strongly felt. For example, the Indian nationalist movement, which achieved Indian Independence, began at the National People's Congress, and it has not changed the traditional beliefs of the Indian people even though many people were involved in the movement. As a result, deeply embedded religious beliefs combined with a Western ideology of democracy have formed the current values of the Indian people. These values have made Indians satisfied with their present lives or mobilized them to improve their lives through individual or family efforts, which are not likely to be interfered with or challenged by the government. In China, however, people value order, equality, and collective efforts, which are seen to be more favorable to population control.

With different traditional values concerning population, Chinese society seems more conducive to its control. Without an established religion, the position of god in many religious people's minds was occupied by the emperor who was regarded as the Son of Heaven and whose edicts were never supposed to be questioned in traditional Chinese society. Now, while all the emperors are dead and gone, the government possesses the highest power in influencing or shaping people's behaviors, and people are likely to accept the values and ideas proposed by the government. As the values of collectivism, equality, and selflessness are combined with the traditional emphasis on order and obedience, the Chinese people show an inclination to follow instructions issued by the central government (Wang, 1999). Therefore, the Chinese have not inherited a strong religion or strong traditional values that may have prevented them from practicing family planning or having abortions. While the traditions that encourage people to have more children have considerably weakened by rapidly increasing urbanization and Western individualism, the Chinese population has changed dramatically from that of India.

On the other hand, that the Indian people value tolerance, asceticism, purification, rituals, democracy, and individual or family efforts is not a good basis for population control, especially in less developed rural areas where population is more likely to be seen as a problem from a collectivist point of view or when all society is taken into consideration. Normally, population control requires individuals to sacrifice their present interest for the long-term public good. India has adopted a Western political system based on traditional values and religious organizations. It functions like a Western society with a democratic political system but is actually powered by religious beliefs and the traditional values. In Indian society, if anything would reduce population growth, it would be economic development and the economic development-induced urbanization.

Ethnicity and Language Differences

Other factors that contributed to differences in population control policy adoption, policy implementation, and population change are ethnicity and language. Generally speaking, China has a homogeneous population, a unified language, and a tightly organized society. India has a heterogeneous population, plural languages, and a highly diversified and loosely knit society. These differences have contributed to how the two societies function differently.

Since China has been a unified nation throughout most of its history and Chinese culture has had a strong presence in its long history, most Chinese have shared the same history and language. In India, many different ethnic groups or cultures exist side by side, and the Indian subcontinent had never actually been unified, India is really a hodgepodge society with many different ethnic groups and over a thousand languages, each with its distinct script, grammar, vocabulary, and literary traditions (Guha, 2007).

When the PRC was established in 1949, the country became highly unified again, although it has experienced more than a century of invasion, civil wars, chaos, and division. To mobilize its population to develop the economy, in the 1950s the government started a Wipe-Out Illiteracy Campaign to increase the literacy rate and improve communications throughout the vast nation. At the same time, the Chinese government simplified traditional Chinese characters and promoted Mandarin as a standardized pronunciation form in 1956. As a result, the literacy rate in China increased substantially from about 20% in 1950 to about 97% in 2020 (CIA, 2020). The vast majority of Chinese, including many minorities, speak Mandarin and understand each other.

When India was under British colonial control, English was used for official purposes at the federal level and in many areas. When India obtained its independence in 1947, it still had more than 560 kingdoms or princely states, which had different religions, cultures, and languages. The new Republic of India did not even possess a language that can be used as a national language. Without English, even the nationalist leaders, such as Patel, Bose, Nehru, Gandhi, and Ambedkar would not be able to communicate with each other. In fact, the Indian population speaks over a thousand languages, although the official language for Indians is Hindi with English as an additional language for government work. After Independence, the Indian Constitution, adopted in 1950, expected the gradual adaptation of Hindi as India's official language to replace English over a period of 15 years. However, the Indian constitution also gave the Indian parliament the power to use English continuously even after the 15-year period.

The Indian National Assembly finally agreed to make Hindi in the Devanagari script the official language of the Union in 1963. However, when an attempt was made to replace English by Hindi in 1964, it was met by strong resistance by non-Hindi-speaking states. As a result, English has been retained as an official language along with Hindi. At the state level, the state government has the power to legislate its own official languages. Consequently, different states in India may use different languages as their state official language and the Indian government has recognized 18 official languages, with Hindi as the most widely spoken language. Communications between states with different official languages may use English translation to accompany documents in their official languages (Guha, 2007).

Different from India, today's China has a territory of about 9.6 million square kilometers and about 1.40 billion people. Among its population, there are 56 officially recognized ethnic groups and about 92% of the population are Han Chinese. Among the minorities, most look similar to the Han population, the colors of their skins are similar to that of the majority population, and it is not always easy to make distinctions between majority and minorities. Within this population, Mandarin has been widely used not only by the majority Han Chinese but also by many minorities. The largest minority in China is Zhuang, about 1.3% of China's population. Although many minorities in China have their own languages, most also speak Mandarin or communicate with people in other ethnic groups easily with Mandarin. Some Han people in China may speak Mandarin in local dialects; however, the written form of Mandarin is the same. After many years of promoting a national pronunciation standard, the number of people who understand only their local dialects has been substantially reduced.

Different from China, today's India has a territory of about 3.3 million square kilometers, a little less than a third of China's size, and about 1.4 billion population. Among the Indian population, 72% are Indo-Aryans, 25% are Dravidians, 3% are Mongoloids, and others. Physically, the Indian population may represent the world, some look European, some look Asian, and others look African. Among the diversified Indian population, about 43.6% speak Hindi, 8% speak Bengali, 6.9% speak Marathi, 6.7% speak Telugu, 5.7% speak Tamil, 4.6% speak Gujarati, 4.2% speak Urdu, 3.6% speak Kannada, 3.1% speak Odia, 2.9% speak Malayalam, 2.7% speak Punjabi, 1.3% speak Assamese, 1.1% speak Maithili, and 5.6% speak other languages (CIA, 2022b).

Chinese society has a much more unified language, and it is a lot easier for the Chinese to communicate with each other and understand each other than for Indians to do the same. This difference is an important factor that affects the functioning of the two societies and may have contributed to the differences in population control policy adoption and implementation in the two societies. What is more, a language also indicates a unique culture. When a society speaks the same language, people in the society may share many social values and can communicate with each other easily. When a society speaks many different languages, it also has many different social values and it becomes much more difficult to communicate with each other. This is exactly the difference between China and India, and this difference may explain other differences between the two societies. Naturally, it is easier for China to adopt a population control policy and implement it throughout the nation.

Social Class Differences

Socially, Indian society is much more divided than Chinese society. Traditionally, India is a society with a caste system that divides the Indian population into five groups. Caste was derived from the Portuguese casta, and it means race, lineage, or breed. At the top of the caste hierarchy are Brahmins, who are priests and teachers. On the second level is the Kshatriya, whose social roles include landholders, warriors, and rulers. On the third level is the Vaishya, who traditionally were businessmen. These three upper castes constitute roughly 15% of India's population today and have ruled India for more than 3,000 years. On the fourth level is the Shudra, which includes laborers and artisans. About 50% of Indians belong to the Shudra caste, which is further divided into hundreds of sub-castes. Below these four levels are the Dalits, untouchables or scheduled castes and tribes. About 20% of Indians belong to this group. The remaining 15% belong to other religions, such as Islam, the Sikh religion, Christianity, and Zoroastrianism (Das, 2002). In traditional India, untouchables were prohibited to talk, touch, or even come in contact with people from a higher caste. Of course, they never had a chance to move up the social ladder. The caste system was formed in India more than 3,000 years ago, and it was the yoke of Indian society. It is a large factor in maintaining Indian society's stability or stagnation.

The religious explanation of the caste system is that each group of the caste system was from a different part of the Brahma's body. The first caste or the

Brahmins were created from Brahma's head; the second caste or the Kshatriyas were from Brahma's arms; the third were the Vaishyas from Brahma's thighs; and the fourth caste was the Shudras, originating from Brahma's feet. Outside of the caste were the Dalits. The caste of a person determined not only his/her job but also his/her social life and what kind of person he/she can marry. During the British colonial period, the colonial government utilized the caste system as a convenient tool to control Indian society, which has actually made the caste system worse in India. When the British Raj started to take power in India, their exploitation of the caste system actually made the British allied with the Brahmin caste and restored some of its privileges that had already been repealed by the Muslim rulers (Szczepanski, 2020)

After India's independence, the new government made the caste system illegal. During the 1950s, the Indian government wanted to break the caste system through land reform to liberate lower-class people so that India could develop more fully. The new Indian Constitution also provided a framework with strategies to enforce equality, provide preferential treatment of the depressed classes, and provide resources and benefits to bridge the gap between the non-privileged castes or tribes and the privileged classes or castes.

However, improvements in the lives of the scheduled castes and tribes are quite limited. Ten years of efforts in land reform made only the richest farmers sell limited amounts of land to less rich farmers, who could not make any significant changes to Indian society. Today, "the fact remains that half a century after Independence, the Dalits and some of the backward castes are still the most wretchedly poor, the most illiterate, the most exploited, and the most disadvantaged in India" (Das, 2002: 147). The reality is as Guha has stated as follows:

> Far from disappearing with democracy and modernization, caste continued to have a determining influence in (and on) Indian society. In town or village, at leisure or at work, most Indians were defined by the endogamous group into which they were born.
>
> (Guha, 2007: 598)

Even among those who immigrate to the United States, the caste system still affects inter caste marriage decisions.

Das has also described how the caste system maintains its hold on Indian society, especially in the rural areas:

> when I began to travel in rural areas for Vicks, I realized that caste indeed was the central organizing feature of social life in the countryside, even though the educated middle and upper middle classes in the cities tended to gloss over it. Caste seemed to divide Indian society into groups whose members did not intermarry and usually did not eat with each other, their status decided by who would and would not take water from the other's hand. Every one within a caste was a brother, and outside it a stranger. Caste varied

> by region, and the relative position of the castes differed from village to village. But everywhere caste rules were rigid, and there was little room for individuality.
>
> (Das, 2002: 140)

A fundamental factor that prevented the improvement of the lower caste was that the socioeconomic conditions that were cultivated by the caste system and supported the caste system continued to exist, although there are some changes. For example, while about 10% of Brahmins continued their traditional roles in religious services, most have become the upper class of the new society, occupying positions such as government officials, lawyers, doctors, and professors. Similarly, many of the Kshatriyas have become large landlords and high-ranking military officials. They exert great influence on central and local governments. Similarly, the Vaishyas have dominated business and industry.

The lower castes, the Shudras and the Dalits, make up about 70% of the Indian people, and the government has adopted measures similar to affirmative action policies in the United States to improve the social status of the lower castes. What makes things worse for the lower-caste population is that they are further divided into thousands of sub-divisions and each sub-group feels superior to some other sub-groups, and each discriminates against other subgroups. Social violence does not occur only between different social castes but also between different subgroups, which may have considerably affected the lower castes' ability to improve their social status.

Today, there are still two traditionally disadvantaged social groups in Indian society: One is the scheduled castes (the untouchables), and the other is the scheduled tribes. These two disadvantaged groups have about 24% of the Indian population, with the percentage increasing since Independence. The scheduled castes and tribes are from different religious groups. Some practice Buddhism, some practice Sikhism, others practice Hinduism, and still others practice Christianity or Zoroastrianism.

In Indian society today, while the caste system has remained a fundamental and important source of social identification for most people, it is still the base of social morality and behavior. Therefore, Indian society is highly divided and social progress seems often blocked by the caste system. Those who belong to the lower caste believe that suffering is their fate and the children of the untouchables will be always untouchables. Such a mentality has actually helped maintain the caste system. At the same time, the democratic political system seems also to have solidified the caste system. Political elections often allow the caste system to change from a personal identification system into groups of people with different political interest (Wu, 2002). When political elections make the traditional caste instrumental, the caste system acquires new functions in Indian society.

Similarly, Chinese society was also rigidly classified during China's early history, such as in the Zhou Dynasty between 1046 BCE and 774 BCE. At that time, the king and the nobles were at the top of the society. On the second social ladder were the warriors and government leaders. The artisans were at the middle of the society. The farmers were the lower middle class, and the slaves were at the bottom of the society.

During the 2,132 years between the Qin Dynasty (221–206 BCE) and the Qing Dynasty (1636–1911 CE), Chinese society was usually divided into four classes or four occupations with the emperor and his family ruling all of them. These four classes include *Shi* (scholars), *Nong* (farmers), *Gong* (artisans and craftsmen), and *Shang* (merchants). *Shi* was at the top of the social hierarchy, and they served in various roles as government officials, clerks, advisors, and overseers. This group was about 10% of the population. *Nong* was on the second level, and they usually farmed in the fields and provided grain for the society and revenues for the government. The *Nong* group was the majority of the society and often made up of about 80% of the population. Then, *gong* was on the third tier and they worked either for the government or on their own. Their skills and contributions to society determine their position in society. *Shang* was at the bottom because they actually did not produce anything but gained profits through the transition of other people's products. *Gong* and *Shang* groups usually comprised about 10% of the Chinese population.

Traditional Chinese social classification indicated the importance or social values that the government and Chinese society attached to each group of people in the society, or was more political than financial, for *gong* and *shang* could be richer than *nong* in real life and the real position of *shang* in the traditional Chinese society could change when they accumulate more wealth. Although many people inherited the occupations from their parents and the change of social status was difficult, there was always an opportunity for social mobility.

Of course, the kings, or the emperor and his family were always at the top of Chinese society and their positions were normally inherited. There were slaves in Chinese society, but they were often prisoners who turned into slaves or the extremely poor people who might sell themselves to the rich family to become an indentured slave. In many circumstances, one was not born into slavery status and could change it. For example, an indentured slave could be free again if he or she worked out his or her terms. Similarly, when the individuals in the *gong* or *shang* group donated substantial amount of their wealth to the government, they could move into the gentry or upper class. At the same time, anyone who could pass the government-organized examinations could move into a higher class or even the upper class with his family.

Since the Tang Dynasty (618–907 CE), the government officials were no longer hereditary and they were selected through government-organized examinations. Although the rich and official families were privileged, the official examination was open to anyone in Chinese society and some lower-class Chinese passed the exams and moved onto the upper level of the society with their families. Many of those scholars who passed the rigid government-organized examinations actually became an important part of the Chinese government bureaucracy.

After the Chinese Communist revolution and the establishment of the PRC in 1949, Chinese society became a highly equal society, with rich landlords' property seized and divided among all the poor farmers in the rural areas and the corporations and private business in the urban areas were nationalized, symbolically purchased by the government. When almost everyone worked for the government, for the state-owned business or collectively owned People's Communes, they either received salaries from the state-owned organizations or working points from the People's Communes, their incomes were different but within a very small range. Under the Chinese economic system between the 1950s and 1970s, Chinese society had become even more homogenous and tightly organized, within which the government's implementation of its policies was extremely effective. That is why China was able to adopt and carry out its population control policy very effectively during the 1970s.

However, after the reforms started in 1978, Chinese society privatized many state-owned corporations in the urban areas and disbanded most of the People's Communes in the rural areas. As a result, the social inequality increased substantially and the gap between the poor and the rich has been large. Nevertheless, the social mobility in Chinese society is much greater than that in Indian society, for many of the top company executives or owners are from the bottom of the Chinese society.

Although both Chinese and Indian societies were hierarchical either in the past or at present, the Chinese social hierarchy has never been as rigid as that of Indian society. In the traditional Indian society, people's social status was determined when they were born and their predetermined social status would determine their occupation and what roles to play in the society. Contrary to Indian society, in the traditional Chinese society, what roles people play determined their social status and an individual's social status may change through individual efforts, such as passing the different levels of the government-organized examinations.

The Chinese have never developed a class system as rigid as that of the caste system in India, and most of the time, social mobility has always been greater in Chinese society than in Indian society. One implication of the rigid social stratification in India is that people became a member of or had to stay within their social caste and many Indians lack the ideology of equality and therefore are less likely to try to improve their social status. On the other hand, the Chinese are much more likely to try to move on to a higher social class through hard work or uprising if social mobility was totally blocked. That is probably why Indian society seems more stable or more stagnant than Chinese society. On the other hand, that is also why competition in Chinese society has always been severe and social conflicts easily get out of control.

An important implication to the population control here is that when Indian society is highly divided and stratified, it is much more difficult to adopt and implement a population control policy that runs basically against individual interests or preference. Within India's democratic political system, people in each caste do not want to see their population decrease or grow slower than other castes, for more people means more votes or more power in the society when the caste system has become instrumental in elections. Although the Indian government fixed, until the year 2001, the number of members of Parliament and members of the Legislative

Assembly on the basis of the census of 1971, it could not prevent people from trying to expand their voting numbers through population increase.

In contrast to India, China's homogenous and less stratified society is more conducive to adopting and implementing population control policies because the policies were applied to everyone and the whole society benefitted from controlled population growth. Also, in a more equal society, it is easier for the government to adopt and implement a policy that is expected to benefit the whole society.

Family Differences

With different traditional values and religions; with different social structures, families in India have more functions than do the families in China. While the government's administrative power is weak in India, the functions of family or lineage system are strong. The family and the endogamous groups called *jatis* are responsible for each member for almost everything, and each member's life, from birth to death, is within the family system. Contrary to the loose organization of Indian society, the Indian families and *jatis* are tightly organized and their members are highly dependent on each other.

The traditional family is based on an extended or joint family system. In Indian families, the oldest male member is the absolute head, under whose roof his younger brothers and their families, his sons, their wives and children, and grandchildren all live. The whole family eats food cooked in one kitchen, holds property in common, and performs religious rituals together. Such a family in India is the most important organization to each family member, and it is a multipurpose organization within which a great many activities are carried out. Specifically, "the family is the principal unit of economic production as well as of consumption. Land is owned and worked by families. The exchange of goods and services in the traditional manner is largely between families of different *jatis*" (Mandelbaum, 1970: 41).

In terms of religious activities, the family is a unit before god. In almost every house, there is a special place for the holy things that help guard all in the household. In fact, most of the religious rituals are held in families. Socially, a family not only is a reproductive unit and a socialization agency but also provides each person with his/her main link to the wider society. Kinship ties are generally taken to be the most durable, reliable, worthy, and moral of all social relations (Mandelbaum, 1974). Most important, the family is the only insurance people can fall back on when they are old or unable to support themselves.

This family pattern, although more and more influenced by urbanization and modernization, remains in both cities and rural areas in India, because the more functions a family has, the more important it is. Or the more important it is, the more functions it may have. In this case, the interest of the family is much more important than anything else, the relationships between family members or lineage members are intense. That is probably why the rate of arranged marriage is about 90% in India (Zuckerman, 2020), which is higher than most other societies. At the same time, relationships outside the family or the lineage are weak.

In the past century, India has changed a great deal. Sophisticated transportation and communication systems keep the states and regions in touch with central and state governments. Most lower-class people, however, are not strongly influenced by the central government. The structure of the Indian family may not be directly responsible for high fertility in India, but it gives the Indian government more difficulties in implementing its policies, especially a policy like family planning, which may harm family interests in rural areas.

Different from the Indian families, the traditional Chinese family has been the center of society, and it is closely related to the state at the same time. For example, the state in Chinese is literally a combination of two words: state and family, or state-family. Historically, the emperor was perceived as the Son of Heaven, and citizens under the emperor's rule were seen as child-citizens. Similarly, the relationship between administrators and citizens was often viewed as equivalent to parents and children. For example, citizens may be referred to as sons and daughters of government administrators, and government administrators may be referred to as parent officials. Compared to Western parents, Chinese parents have much greater power over their children and much greater responsibility for their children. Similarly, the Chinese government has much more power over its citizens and much more responsibility for its citizens.

Similarly, Chinese society is perceived as a big family. Accordingly, friends, neighbors, or even acquaintances are perceived as or referred to as family members or relatives. Persons within the same generation may refer to each other as brothers or sisters, and persons in an older generation may be uncles or aunts or grandpas or grandmas. Accordingly, many behaviors in a family are also seen in society. For example, younger persons are expected to respect elders. Therefore, the seniors are more likely to be respected than in many other societies while a community or the society is perceived as a family.

Although traditional Chinese families or clans are similar to those of the Indian families or *jatis*, they have changed substantially in China in the past century. Ever since the May Fourth Movement in 1919, traditional family values have been blamed for the backwardness of Chinese society. As a result, family functions declined in number when China launched nationwide socialist reforms after the founding of the PRC. After the nationalization of urban companies and corporations in the 1950s, family ownership of private industrial and commercial organizations virtually disappeared, which reduced the importance of families in urban areas. Similarly, after the collectivization of land in rural areas and after the establishment of the People's Communes in rural areas during the latter 1950s, the importance of families has declined in rural areas. These fundamental changes in both urban and rural areas were partly due to widespread collectivism in traditional Chinese society and further reduced by the individualism of current Chinese society.

During the 1960s and 1970s, a few political movements directly or indirectly reduced family values and family functions further. They underlined the Chinese government's efforts to further cultivate collectivism and reduce private individual values. While working organizations in urban areas and People's Communes in rural areas were responsible for individuals' employment, education, housing, health care, and retirement, the importance and functions of the traditional family were further reduced.

The introduction of new collective production or socialist practices gradually changed the relationship between family and society, and between family and individuals. In both cities and rural areas, the family was no longer a production unit. Workers worked for state-owned factories, peasants produced for production teams, and each received payment directly from their working organizations or production teams for their work. The family was no longer a unit of trade, for all the products of factories and production teams were sold to the state at a standard price. When a person was ill or no longer able to support himself or herself, he or she could depend on the factory or the production team he or she had worked for. The family was no longer the only agency that provided help to those who needed it. A person's life mostly depended on the prosperity of the country, factories, and production teams. In this case, when the functions of the family were getting fewer, the size of families was getting smaller. The family and individuals were less important than the country. In such a society, social norms were easily established and internalized. Peer pressure was always strong, which kept everyone in line. This social condition kept the enormous Chinese population together, but also prevented different ideas from prevailing and gave the Chinese government a favorable atmosphere in which to carry out population control policies.

Economic reforms started in the later 1970s, privatizing many state-owned companies and restoring the importance and functions of traditional families in urban areas. Similarly, disbanding People's Communes and privatizing land in rural areas restored the importance and functions of the traditional family to farmers. This is a reason why family planning programs were more difficult to implement in China during the 1980s.

However, the restored importance of the traditional family was soon reduced by socioeconomic development and the rapid urbanization of Chinese society. Economic reforms begun at the end of the 1970s released pent-up individual desires for wealth. This time, it was the individual striving for a better life and wealth that affected Chinese families. For example, seeking a better paying job or better opportunities to get rich motivated farmers to leave their families in rural areas to work as temporary employees or start a business in urban areas, which left family members separated for a long period of time. From urban and rural areas, Chinese even went to other countries to seek better education and opportunity, leaving family members behind for many years. Individuals striving for career or wealth improved education, improved life, increased wealth, and raised the expectations of individual Chinese; however, along with rapid urbanization, traditional family values and functions have been reduced because the cost of forming a family or raising a child has been substantially increased and many young people would rather enjoy their individual lives than raise a family. Even after the Chinese government adopted a new two-children-per-couple policy in 2016 and again a new policy of three-children-per-couple policy in 2021, few couples have had more than one child.

The roles or functions associated with families always exert an impact on human reproduction. Thus, when the family has many functions, it tends to be important and large; however, when the family has fewer functions, it becomes less important and smaller. Similarly, when the family may increase individual opportunities to develop or promote individual wellbeing, the family tends to be larger. On the other hand, when large families impede individual opportunities to develop and reduce individual wellbeing, family size tends to be smaller. When an individual's development in the urban areas depends more and more on individual efforts rather than family support, family ties weaken, family size reduces, and birth rates go down. That is another reason why China's population increase rate has fallen much more rapidly than it has in India during the past seven decades.

Another factor influencing population control is child marriage. Before Indian Independence in 1947 and the establishment of the People's Republic of China in 1949, child marriage was common in both societies. In India, child marriage was practiced for centuries. During the Medieval period, girls could get married as young as six or eight years. In China, getting married young was popular; for example, the legal minimum age for marriage was 14 for women and 16 for men during the Qing Dynasty between 1644 and 1911. Early marriage was normally encouraged in traditional China (Xia and Zhou, 2003).

Post 1949 in China, new marriage laws restricted the legal marriage age to 18 years for women and 20 years for men, effectively reducing child marriages. During the 1970s when China started effectively controlling its population growth, the authorized marriage age was increased to 23 for women and 25 for men in rural areas, and 25 for women and 27 for men in urban areas. However, after the reforms started in the later 1970s, child marriages began to increase as traditional patriarchal norms resumed their influence on Chinese society as the government influences reduced. According to research by Fan, Qian, and Koski (2022), child marriage increased from 2.41% in 2000 to 2.85% in 2010 among women and from 0.54% to 0.77% among men, which means that roughly 1.8 million women and 0.5 million men, mostly in the western provinces of China, married before the legal age of 18 years. The area difference indicates different levels of socioeconomic development and different legal marriage age for minorities (some minorities may marry at a younger age). On the other hand, gender differences indicate gender inequality in China.

In India, child marriages are still practiced widely although they are decreasing in many communities. Child marriage was actually institutionalized in the Hindu religion by ascribing a good deal of *punya* [merit] to parents who gave their daughter in prepubertal marriage to an eligible bachelor. During the past century, many efforts have been made to prevent child marriage. In 1929, the British brought in the Child Marriage Restraint Act to restrict the practice of child marriages. After the independence and adoption of the Indian Constitution in 1950, the legislation has been revised several times. The Hindu Marriage Act passed in 1955 specified the minimum age for girls at 18 and 21 for boys. The Act, however, was restricted to Hindu marriages only (Srinivasan, 2017).

The efforts to stop child marriage in India seem to be working but not as expected. According to censuses in 1981, 1991, 2001, and 2011, the percentage of women married before the age of 18 was 43.4% in 1981%, 35.3% in 1991,

14.4% in 2001, and 3.5% in 2011. Although the percentage of child marriages has decreased, girls marrying before 18 are still widely prevalent in many parts of India. Many are child marriages but, fearing prosecution, may not be reported as such. In parts of rural and urban India, child marriages increased between 2001 and 2011 (Srinivasan, 2017).

After a comprehensive study of India's population trends, policies, and programs, Professor Srinivasan has pointed out that the continued prevalence of child marriages is a major problem that India needs to address. Even in states like Tamil Nadu and Kerala where marriage age for girls has been relatively high, there are pockets in the state where child marriages are still prevalent. Although the custom of arranged marriages cannot be changed through national policies and programs, child marriage should be prevented by law (2017).

Punishment for child marriage seems severe in India. For example, the punishment for a male between 18 and 21 marrying a child was imprisonment of up to 15 days or a fine of Rs. 1,000, or both. Similarly, the punishment for a male above 21 years marrying a minor was an imprisonment of up to 3 months and a possible fine. In addition to the punishment of those who married a minor, the punishment for anyone who performed or directed a child marriage ceremony was an imprisonment of up to 3 months and a possible fine. The punishment for a parent or guardian of a child taking part in the child marriage was imprisonment of up to 3 months and/or a possible fine (Srinivasan, 2017).

Before social customs can be fundamentally changed or before family functions become substantially reduced, child marriage will be a social problem in India. At the same time, child marriage will continue to contribute more to population growth in India than in China. Similarly, differences in child marriage between China and India will contribute to different population changes in the two societies because child marriage shortens the span of generations and contributes to population growth.

Differences in Social Status and the Education of Women

Another important difference that contributes to the relative success of population control in India and China is the status of women and their typical levels of education. In China and India, women's status was always lower than men's, and they occupied the lowest position in families. Considered inferior to men, women were often seen as their husbands' property or slaves.

In traditional China, women had lower status, and the key female characteristic was obedience: to obey fathers when young, husbands when married, and adult sons when widowed. "Throughout their lives, women were supposed to be only slightly more than chattel, routinely bought and sold in marriage, concubinage or outright slavery" (Johnson, 1983: 1). For more than 2,000 years, husbands were the masters of their wives. A man could marry many times and have several wives if he could afford them. But a woman could have only one husband and marry once. If her husband died, she was supposed to remain a widow for the rest of her life. If she committed suicide when her husband died to show her faith to him, she would be praised highly.

Similarly, in traditional India, women were treated much the same. According to Mandelbaum, "women, whether in the status of daughter, wife or widow, are entitled to maintenance by their male kin, but under the ancient law, they had no other vested rights in the family property" (1970: 35). Following the laws of Manu, which became the canon law of Hinduism, a husband must be constantly worshiped as a god by a faithful wife. He cannot be displaced even though he is devoid of good qualities, addicted to evil passion, fond of spirituous liquors, or diseased. An old terrible custom to indicate women's social status in traditional India is that when the husband died, the wife would be burned to death at her husband's funeral.

In 1949, the social status of Chinese women changed completely. The Marriage Law, passed in 1950, constitutionally provided women the same equal rights as men traditionally had. It was of great importance to the movement for women's liberation in China. The basic principle of the law was to abolish the arbitrary and compulsory traditional marriage system based on the superiority of men. It was based on the free choice of partners, equal rights for both sexes, and social protection of the legal interests of women and children. The implementation of the new Marriage Law also shifted the center of the family from the parents to the two married partners. Fundamental changes in family organization, in the long run, proved to be one of the most important foci of a shift to a democratic organization of Chinese society (Parsons, 1959).

In 1953, the central government of China deliberately launched a mass movement to enforce the new marriage law and get rid of the still-existing tradition that repressed women for hundreds of years. At the same time, the abolition of private business and the socialization of the means of production began to bring women into productive labor outside of the family. When women were put into an independent economic position, their economically dependent status changed. Between 1950 and the 1970s, the Chinese government repeatedly carried out extensive educational programs to preserve the new marriage law and encouraged trade unions and women's associations to protect women's rights and interests.

Between the 1950s and 1970s, women in China experienced a dramatic qualitative change in their status. When women in China were viewed as equal to men, their functions in politics, economics, education, and social activities became indispensable. As many people in China said, "women hold up half the sky." With this change, women began enjoying high social and family status. They participated freely in social and political activities, took part in production, and were guaranteed by law the same rights as men in every aspect of political, economic, and social life. If a woman was doing the same kind of job as a man, she usually got the same pay and enjoyed the same opportunity to be promoted. During these three decades, almost no occupation was closed to women, although sometimes, their numbers in some occupations like engineering and heavy industry were still small. There were women ministers, women professors, women governors, women party secretaries, and women pilots. According to the census taken in 1982, the employment rate of women in China was the highest in the world (Ma and Zha, 1984; Wu, 1986).

These changes, making husband and wife equal, have had a great impact upon the life of Chinese families. In both the cities and rural areas, both husband and wife work inside and outside of the house. Both are responsible for family income, and both share housework. In 1982, the monthly national family average income was 135.08 yuan, of which 42.2 percent were contributed by wives (Family, 1985). Because both are responsible, the decision making of a family is totally in the hands of husband and wife. Between the 1950s and 1970s, if a woman felt that she had been maltreated by her husband, she might go to her work unit leader or her husband's to ask for help. If she failed to get help from those units, she might go to the women's association, which was always ready to step in and back up woman's rights.

During the 1960s and 1970s, many people in China believed that women were as important and as intelligent as men. If a woman happened to be their leader, they were willing to obey her. Most women believed that they were not men's tools whose function was to produce children, and they were confident that they were as good as men. Therefore, everywhere in China, women were confidently competing with men. The consequence of this was that it required them to spend a lot of their time on their career development rather than on raising children one after another. Their attitude made Chinese women more willing to practice family planning and have fewer children.

Similar to China, women's status improved in India after Independence when Indian women rose to fight against men's cruelties—when women opposed polygamy, sought the right to divorce, claimed equality in marital rights, and demanded restrictions on dowries. Accordingly, the Indian Constitution guarantees certain rights to women. For example, women have been granted equal rights in politics; they can be appointed to the highest office of the state on the basis of constitutionally provided equal opportunity. They also have the legal right to choose education and professional training to enable entry to careers. Indian government policies also prohibit any kind of discrimination based on gender. A Dowry Prohibition Act was adopted in 1961 and amended in 1984 to control dowries. In politics, women's status has improved considerably. Generally speaking, women's status has improved and is better in the South than in the North, and their status has improved more in urban than in rural areas (Ranjan, 1999).

Efforts in uplifting women in India were mostly, however, in the field of law, and women's status has been improved on paper more than in reality. For example, the Hindu Marriage Act of 1955 provided equal rights to women to obtain a divorce and remarry, the Hindu Adoption and Maintenance Act of 1956 provided a woman the equal right to adopt a boy or a girl as her son or daughter, and the Hindu Women's Right to Property Act of 1973 gives a woman, either as a daughter, a widow, or a mother the right to inherit the property of the deceased. Similarly, many programs and schemes were formed to bring about progress among women (Kapur, 2019; Mahla, 2021). Despite the laws, treaties, and declarations, the status of women has not been given much recognition, and they are still treated as inferior to men. Those laws do not and cannot change women's status fundamentally when traditional religious beliefs, social biases, and socioeconomic conditions remain.

Although independence from Britain brought many changes, the basic cultural orientation toward men and women in contemporary Indian society is much like it was before. According to Dube (1963), social developments in the past have brought about some modifications in the social status of women; however, covert social norms have not changed to any appreciable extent. Women are still possessed by their husbands, and they do not possess equal rights either inside or outside of their families. Even though developments in social and economic aspects have improved their living conditions, women are still mainly playing the traditional roles of daughter, wife, and mother. This is especially true in upper strata rural families and traditional upper strata urban families.

In those upper-class families, the separate spheres of activity for men and women are clearly distinguished. Men are not expected to undertake women's work, and women are not supposed to do men's jobs. Men's responsibility is in society while women's is at home. Thus, the opportunities for women to work outside of their homes are quite limited. Since traditional ideas regarding men and women are still quite strong in India, those women who enter the professions and social services face severe prejudices. Their work outside of the family is seldom encouraged by society or their families. Of those women who are presently employed in cities as teachers, clerks, or nurses, most are from the middle or upper classes.

Women enter careers not because they want them but because there is nothing else for them to do until their parents find them husbands. In this situation, these employed women are not treated or paid equally. They are usually neither capable of nor expected to compete with men. Of course, this is not a problem to most people, for in many people's minds in India, earning and giving economic support to the family is not a woman's primary responsibility. Instead, women are expected to depend on their families or their husbands. This dependence unavoidably deprives them of equal status. When traditional religious beliefs and social biases are not fundamentally changed, women's status cannot be fundamentally improved.

In most Indian families, the husband is expected to assert his superiority over the family scene by controlling and keeping his wife and children under discipline. The wife, instead of struggling for an equal position, usually obeys her husband. With regard to the decision making within extended families, it is often not in the hands of the young husband or the wife. Instead, older family members will make decisions for them.

But even though family traditions in India are rigid and strong, changes have already begun in the cities. In some urban nuclear families, women may work for economic gain, and their share of earnings materially improves the budget of their families. In those families, authority is shared more or less equally by husbands and wives. Gradually, many people are beginning to realize that the entrance of women into the professions and services is inevitable, and a working wife is economically advantageous. As time goes on, the traditional concepts regarding the place and roles of women are slowly changing in India. Those changes, though very slow, seem unavoidable in the future, and they will probably open new horizons for Indian women. Recently, the number of women who participate in national and local politics is increasing. This phenomenon may further improve women's status in Indian society. However, when a woman takes a responsible position and associates with people outside of her family, especially with other men, she is usually frowned upon.

Women's status in China was much better than in India between the 1950s and 1970s. China's reforms in the later 1970s, however, have not only brought in market mechanisms into economic development but also attached greater importance to money or the possession of wealth. When competition increases, the social value of money also increases. With the marketization of the labor force, women face discriminations in some private organizations. In family formation, many marriages have become highly commercialized, and many women are willing to be bought into wealthy families. As a result, women's equal status has been compromised, and many women are willing to give up their equal status in exchange for material possessions. Many men achieved their superior status over women with their money or wealth. At the same time, the social mechanisms that guaranteed equal status for women have been weakened. Worse still, prostitution which had disappeared from Chinese society for about three decades after the PRC's founding returned in the 1980s.

Nevertheless, women's status in today's China is much better than that in India. For example, there are fewer Indian women to participate in international athletic competitions, but Chinese women often perform better than Chinese men in those competitions. Between 1984 and 2016, Chinese women athletes won 55% of the gold medals awarded to Chinese athletes at the summer Olympic Games. Indian women did not win any gold medals during the same period.

Another example is women's success in business. According to Forbes 34th Annual World's Billionaires list in 2020, of the 234 women on the list of 2,095 billionaires listed by Forbes, only 67 are considered "self-made," which, according to Forbes, are those who have built a company or established a fortune on their own. Almost half of these 67 female billionaires are from Greater China, 28 from the mainland, and five from Hong Kong. India, with a population comparable to China, has only two women who created billion-dollar fortunes. Among the ten richest self-made women in the world in 2020, seven are in China, one in Hong Kong, one in the United States, and one in the United Kingdom (Glinska, 2020). This is a strong indicator of Chinese women's strong status in Chinese society.

Similarly, Chinese women seem to have more opportunities than Indian women in national politics. During China's 13th National People's Congress held in 2019, 24.9% of the lawmakers were women. This percentage has exceeded the world average of 24.3% (Di, 2019). In comparison, the proportion of seats held by women in the National Parliaments in India was 14.4% in 2021. In 2000, women's share of the Indian National Parliament seats was 9.0% (Index Mundi, 2022). In 2003, women's percentage of the National People's Congress members was 20.2 in China (Zeng, 2014). In both countries, women's percentage in the national legislation body has been increasing, and Chinese women have a larger share.

Still another example is dowries. The tradition of the bride bringing a dowry to her husband's family at a wedding exists in both China and India, but it is different in the two societies. In Indian society, a dowry is requested not only at the time of wedding but also when the husband's family wants it again after wedding. Dowries may be durable goods, cash, or movable property that the bride's family gives to the groom, his parents, or his relatives as a condition of the marriage in India. Therefore, to have a daughter is a burden for ordinary Indians. In some places, when a daughter is married, the parents must send her with half of their property. If a family has three daughters, it will have to give half of its property three times. In Tamil, there is a popular saying that even a king will become a pauper if he has five daughters (Srinivasan, 2017). This is another reason why women have low social status in India.

According to Algu, dowries in India place an unnecessary financial burden on impoverished families and their daughters. A bride's family typically spends about Rs. 32,000 on a dowry which can be worth as much as several years of household income for a women's family. Some low-income families obtain loans from upper-caste moneylenders at high-interest rates. When they cannot repay the loans, they often enter into bonded labor at the moneylender's service to repay the debt (2021).

Worse still, after marriage, the husband becomes the master of the wife, and he has the right to demand more dowry whenever he feels it necessary. If the wife's family fails to provide more dowry, as the husband's family demands, she may be killed by her husband's family. Every year, women are killed by their husband's family simply because their parents failed to provide more dowry demanded by their husbands.

When the author visited Bangalore in 2006, he was informed by the local women's association that there were about three women killed daily in the city because their parents failed to provide demanded dowries. A commonly used cover-up for the death is that the woman's sari caught fire in a kitchen accident and burned to death. When a woman's parents are suspicious and take the case to a court, there is little chance for them to win the case because the woman's body was cremated before the sun rose and her family was often informed of their daughter's death after their daughter's body was cremated. Sometimes, even when the court takes a case it can take years to have the case processed. Dowries can easily drive families with several daughters into poverty and at the same time keep women in a subordinate status.

Contrary to Indian tradition, the Chinese tradition actually benefits women. When a Chinese girl is engaged or about to have a wedding, the husband's family pays a bride price according to their financial resources, but it has to be acceptable to the bride's family. Such bride prices have increased substantially in the past three decades. On the other hand, the bride will also bring a dowry to the bridegroom's family. The husband and his family normally expect it, but cannot demand it, to say nothing of asking for more after the wedding.

Chinese and Indians have different perspectives on dowry. In India, when a girl is about to marry a man, it is assumed that in the days to come, the husband's family will support her. Therefore, the bride's family should share some of the cost and provide the husband's family with a dowry which may equal half of the wife's family's property. In China, the bride's parents may think that they have raised their daughter and spent more efforts and money on raising her; therefore, they expected a bride price from her future husband or his family. Therefore, the Chinese dowry custom normally benefits the bride's family while the Indian dowry custom normally places a heavy burden on the bride's family.

Since social status is often related to education, it is reasonable to expect that the typical education of women is different in China than that in India. In China, women's opportunities to be educated vary. In the cities, girls and boys enjoy an equal chance to go to school. A school-age child, whether male or female, rarely remains outside of school. Yet in rural areas, even if everybody is eligible to attend state-run or village-run schools, fewer girls than boys attend. This is because of the old traditions that encourage some to think that educating girls is unnecessary or not in the family's best interests, for a married daughter will leave when she grows up.

Among those Chinese girls and boys who go to school, many have the goal of being educated or acquiring knowledge and training for future careers. It is also a commonly shared belief that education leads people to more prestigious and better paying jobs. When many women are well-educated, they also play important roles in China's education, which further increases women's education in the society. For example, the school life expectancy was 14 years in 2015, the same for both males and females. When China's total literacy rate was 96.8% in 2018, the rate was 95.2% for females and 98.5% for males (CIA, 2022a). The gender difference in the literacy rate was 3.3% in China in 2018. As a result of education and equal social status, many young girls in China are very aggressive. When they enter the marriage market, they would rather choose their husband than be chosen as wives.

In India, the opportunities for girls to be educated have increased considerably since Independence; however, the opportunities for girls to be educated are still limited, especially in rural areas. In many rural areas, there is simply no school available. Starting in 1947, the Indian government has tried to set up schools in villages, but they cannot send enough school teachers to work in the villages or keep them working there for a long time. On many occasions even if the schools are available, parents still believe that schooling for girls is a waste. In fact, some even hold to the traditional belief that educated girls are prone to all kinds of misfortune—barrenness, shrewishness, or widowhood (Mandelbaum, 1974).

In more traditional rural areas in India, a young girl usually works in the kitchen with her mother until her marriage. All that is required of her is knowledge of cooking and other domestic chores, the rituals that girls are expected to perform, and respect for and obedience to her parents-in-law and husband. Obviously, knowledge acquired at school is unnecessary. In the cities, educational opportunities for women are available on a limited scale. Therefore, girls from lower-strata urban communities rarely get any education beyond the sixth grade, and higher education is available only to the few from the upper class.

Of those girls who do go to high schools and colleges, many are seeking their education with a view to marriage rather than a career. A bridegroom who has had a good education is prized, and such a young man typically requires his bride also to be educated. As a result, the education of many Indian girls does not prepare them to compete with men on the job market, but prepares them to be chosen by men on the marriage market. As a result, when India's total literacy rate was 74.4% in 2018, that rate was 65.8% for the females and 82.4% for the males (CIA, 2022b). The gender difference was 16.6% in 2018. Consequently, women in China and India have received different levels of education and have different opportunities in their career development. For example, in 2018, the literacy rate was 95.2% for Chinese women and 65.8 for Indian women (CIA, 2022a). The difference in rates between Chinese and Indian women was 29.4% in 2018.

Education is closely related to labor force participation. According to Ortiz-Ospina, Tzvetkova, and Roser (2022), the ratio of female to male labor force participation rate in 2019 was 80.7 in China and 27.4 in India. The female-to-male ratio of time devoted to unpaid care work in 2014 was 9.83 in India and 2.57 in China. According to the Gallop Polls between 2009 and 2012 in China and India, the employment rate was 70% for Chinese women and 25% for Indian women. Among those who received tertiary education, the employment rate was 81% for the Chinese women and 34% for the Indian women. Among those who received secondary education, the employment rate was 69% for the Chinese women and 20% for the Indian women. Similarly, for those who only received primary/early secondary education, the employment rate was 70% for Chinese women and 25% for Indian women (Crabtree and Pugliese, 2012).

> Not only do Indian women participate in the labor force at lower levels, those who do participate have a harder time finding jobs than women in China. Gallup's data indicate that, among Indian women who are labor force participants, 15% are unemployed—meaning they are available for work and looking for jobs—compared with 5% among India's male labor force participants. Among the much larger share of women in the Chinese workforce, 5% are unemployed.
>
> (Crabtree and Pugliese, 2012: 1)

Among those who received higher education, Chinese women's employment rate was similar to that of the Chinese men while Indian women's employment rate was about half of Indian men's (Shrinivasan, 2012). Women's employment rate not only reflects the social status of women but also affects their birth rate. When women have good opportunities to be employed, their birth rate is normally lower (East-West Center, 2002; Ma, 2016). Generally speaking, social status and education are closely related to and complement each other. Thus, more education is seen to lead to higher social status, and higher social status is seen to provide a better chance to be educated. When comparing social status and education in China and India, Chinese women have had a better chance and higher status.

Chinese women's better social status and education have contributed to population control; at the same time, the less equal social status and education of Indian women have hindered India's family planning. When Chinese women have a more equal social and family status, they can themselves help determine the size of their families. At present, their position in the society and at home is mainly determined by how successful they are in their careers, rather than by how many children they have or how many sons they give birth to. On the contrary, the status of Indian women is still affected by how successfully they play the roles of mother and wife, or whether or not they can give birth to enough sons.

At the same time, Chinese women's employment makes them independent. When they are able to work, they do not have to depend on their husbands; when they are retired, they do not have to depend on their children, at least financially. More important, employed women are usually unwilling to spend much of their time and energy raising many children. They can play more roles than wife and mother. But in India, many women are still the dependents of their husbands. The size of their families is often determined by other members of the family. Since many women can play only the roles of mother and wife, they are more willing to, or expected to, give birth to more children.

This is one of the important reasons why India's population control is less effective, as the United Nations Development Programme points out:

> Rapid population growth, high fertility and gender inequality often go hand in hand. Among the countries experiencing rapid population growth, many have high levels of gender inequality expressed in terms of fewer girls than boys going to school, high rates of girls giving birth before reaching adulthood, and fewer women than men in formal employment or political life.
>
> (UNDP, 2020)

Unlike India, China's more equal status for women helped reduce China's population growth. Substantially reduced birth rates and current highly commercialized marriages may, however, pose new problems for Chinese society.

Functional Differences in the Government

Traditionally, highly diversified religious beliefs have divided Indian society, and widely shared Confucianism has been China's social glue. Differences in social structure, language, and tradition have caused differences in government functions in the world's most populous nations.

Ever since Qin Shi Huang unified China and established its hierarchical bureaucracy in China in 221 BCE, its enormous society was mostly under the control of an emperor or a royal family. The emperors' control was through a well-established bureaucratic system, and bureaucrats were selected through official examinations. However, the emperor's control normally did not go below county-level administration in traditional China. Villages in rural areas were virtually administered informally by the gentry who were scholar-officials or prestigious members of the community. Those gentry mostly held Confucian values, which guided them in managing the grassroots level of Chinese society. The gentry informally conciliated disputes between villagers, established and enforced rules or behavior norms, and managed the local community.

Contrary to Chinese society, traditional Indian society was highly divided by religion, language, and caste. For most of Indian history, the subcontinent was divided and controlled by hundreds of princely states or tribes. However, at the grassroots level of Indian society, the Panchayat Raj had informally managed the community. Panchayat normally consisted of five wise and respected elders who were chosen and accepted by the local community. These Panchayats settled disputes between both individuals and villages. They also managed the relationship between the local farmers' community and the state. Because of their important functions, Mahatma Gandhi considered them as the base of democracy. Gandhi believed that the stronger the Panchayats, the happier people would be (You, 2007). This grassroots-level governance was similar to the gentry's management of villages in the traditional China.

Although both societies have changed substantially during the past century, the most basic difference in Chinese and Indian government functions has remained unchanged. After the establishment of the PRC in 1949, China resumed as a tightly organized society, while India, despite Independence, remained a loosely knit society. In India, each state is different from other states and each has its own language, law, and culture. Different from India, the majority of provinces in China speak the same language, obey the same law, and have a similar culture.

In current China, there are 23 provinces, five autonomous regions, four municipalities, and two special administrative regions. Although in some autonomous regions, populated mostly by minorities, people speak different languages, the population in those minority regions is fewer than 9% of China's population, and their government structures are basically the same as other provinces populated by the majority Han population.

Politically speaking, China is a socialist country with one party in control, and politics in China is mostly decided by the Chinese Communist Party. There are about eight small democratic parties that normally cooperate with and supplement the Communist Party. Chinese governance at the top consists of three branches: the central government, the National People's Congress, and the National Political Consultation Conference. These three branches normally cooperate with rather than fight against each other. The Central Committee of the Communist Party has decisive roles in China's national governance. Such a three-branch structure exists in all middle or upper levels of China's governance, including at the national, provincial, prefectural, and county-level governance. At each level, the Communist Party committee is the leading core of governance.

Between the 1950s and 1970s, the CCP Central Committee directed the central government at the highest level. Hierarchical party organizations existed at all levels of government organizations, extending to every social unit, right down to the grassroots level. For example, there was a party branch in every company in the army, every city neighborhood, and every rural village. This means that there was almost no place in China that was out of the party's reach. Accordingly, different echelons of government were the administrative units that carry out the central government's policies. The lowest levels of the government which had the closest contact with the general population were neighborhood committees in the cities and People's Communes in the rural areas. Each neighborhood committee consisted of a number of residence groups. Each committee had several leading groups responsible for such local tasks as civil affairs, security, employment, social services, education, health care, and family planning.

Similarly, in each People's Commune, there were a number of production brigades which contained a number of production teams. The production team was the lowest administrative unit which not only carried out production activities but was also responsible for each commune member's food, health care, education, security, family planning, and care of the aged and disabled. In the rural areas, the traditional gentry management of the villages was first disabled by land reform in the early 1950s and then replaced by the production teams after the establishment of People's Communes later in the 1950s.

Besides these administrative organizations, there were still many kinds of hierarchical formal organizations, such as worker's unions, farmer's unions, youth leagues, women's associations, and militia organizations. Those organizations provided further channels that connected individuals to the central government. Obviously, each individual experienced many influences from many directions because everyone belonged to at least one or two organizations. Accordingly, the whole society was an entity welded together by similar ideology and strongly unified political and economic systems. Such a tight social structure guaranteed the effective implementation of Chinese central government policies, including the population control policy in the early 1970s.

After reforms started in the later 1970s, the structure of Chinese governance changed dramatically. In urban areas, many state-owned companies have been privatized, and many new private companies have also been formed. When the whole society was encouraged to start businesses in the 1980s, many individuals were working on their own businesses. At the same time, the CCP has substantially reduced its functions in state-owned organizations and exited from private companies. In rural areas, most People's Communes were disbanded in the early 1980s, and most agriculture and husbandry in rural areas were privatized. Although CCP organizations still existed in rural areas, their functions were considerably reduced. In other organizations, such as universities, the Communist Party's role was also considerably reduced.

Since the 1980s when the whole country became filled with construction sites, many individual farmers left their villages for jobs as construction workers in urban areas. Those farmers who left their villages and made a living in urban areas were mostly on their own and usually beyond government control. As a result of loosened social control by the Party, large families or strong clans have become dominant in rural areas. In urban areas, large private corporations became influential. The capability of the CCP to carry out its policies has declined considerably.

Before economic reform started in 1978, Party organizations were most complete and could be extremely efficient and effective in carrying out the policies of the central government. Moreover, with the help of the telephone, television, broadcasting systems, and newspapers, those organizations could be mobilized to make the central government's policy known to almost everybody overnight.

After reforms started in 1978, however, Party effectiveness has been reduced. The privatization of production activities in rural areas and the establishment of millions of private organizations in urban areas have substantially reduced CCP influence, although the Party has remained solely in control of the country and society, including population control policies and their implementations. The reduced social control and the absence of the Communist Party organizations in many private organizations had made the family planning programs less effective in the 1980s than in the 1970s, and that is why some local governments, especially at the lower level, had to resort to coercion to keep the birth rate down during the 1980s. Such coercive measures were replaced by economic measures in the 1990s and eventually became unnecessary when rapid economic development and urbanization did their part in reducing the birth rate. At the same time, the implementation of government policies in China has become more indirect and more sophisticated than during the 1980s. Consequently, population control policy has been implemented effectively through either government functioning or rapid socioeconomic development and urbanization.

India, in contrast to China, has a federal-like government structure. Politically, it is a democratic socialism operating in a federation of states and centrally administered union territories. At the top of the power structure is the central, or union, government, which is divided into three major sections: executive, legislative, and judicial. Their functions include passing the laws made by the legislature, making laws and solving conflicts between executive and legislature. The Indian central government has a president, who has the highest executive power, but it is the prime minister who actually administers the central government.

Under the central government, there are 30 states and six union territories, including the National Capital Region of Delhi. The states were formed on the basis of the languages spoken in the area and on the recommendations of the States Reorganization Commission formed in 1950. For administrative purposes, the states and union territories are further divided into districts. A district forms the basic administrative unit for the implementation of the policies and programs of the central and state governments. In 2017, there were 767 districts in India (Srinivasan, 2017).

In China, provincial or local governments are closely related to the central government, and local governments must implement the policies of the central government. However, in India, the central government and the state or district governments are loosely related to each other. Very often, they contradict each other. The differences between different states in India are similar to the differences between different nations in Europe. Like different nations in the world, trade between different states in India is taxed.

In India, from the central government to the local communities, either urban or rural, there are dozens of parties which represent different kinds of ideology and different groups of people. Those parties often contradict, fight, and cancel out each other's strength. Many of these parties have no power at the grassroots level. The result of this multiparty system is that the Indian central government is unlikely to hold or adopt any unpopular policies. If it does adopt an unpopular policy for the long term or the best interest of the nation, it may not last long or may not be effectively implemented. In other words, such a multiparty system can prevent a government from adopting or implementing policies effectively. For example, the Indian population control policy adopted in 1976 recommended the minimum age at marriage of 18 for women and 21 for men. This recommendation was enacted into a law by the government in October 1978. However, the implementation of the law remains weak even after 15 years, and many girls continue to marry below the age of 18 (Srinivasan, 2017).

Today's Indian society is still loosely organized. There are government administrative organizations at the national, state, and district levels, but at the grassroots level, there are no government administrative organizations that bring individuals into direct contact with central government policy implementation. In villages, government agencies carry on police and tax-collecting functions principally, but they have little direct effect on villagers. Other voluntary associations are few in number and limited in purpose, consisting largely of gatherings for religious devotion. Recently, voluntary associations have grown in number and influence, but the change in the organization of the villages is almost negligible. In the cities, many poor people drift from one place to another; no one takes care of them, and no one controls them.

The Panchayat Raj in traditional rural areas was seriously crippled by the British East Indian Company before India's independence. Although both Gandhi and Nehru supported the Panchayat Raj in the rural areas, its real function was limited. A major change to strengthen the Panchayat system was in 1992 when the Panchayati Raj Act was passed. It gave the local Panchayat more authority to function as a self-governance organization. It was believed that local government would be better than centrally appointed bureaucrats in identifying and responding to village needs.

At the same time, varied religious beliefs, a multiparty political system, and a strong private economy provide a more diverse life and make India a loosely organized society under one government. Although nationalism has contributed greatly to India's unification, highly diverse religious beliefs have fundamentally hindered the functioning of government organizations. This phenomenon has clearly demonstrated why the population control in India has been ineffective, as Aspalter points out:

> the absence of strong political institutions constitutes a key explanatory variable for the absence and failure of government policies in the field of social policy. Over the past half a century, India's leading politicians were willing to implement effective population control programs, but failed to do so on the account of fractured political power-bases, as well as the discrepancy between the theory of centrally planned social development and the reality of the federal-structure of Indian democracy.
>
> (Aspalter, 2002: 49)

According to Aspalter, the political system is the major factor contributing to the failure of India's longstanding population control policies. Specifically, he summarized six reasons India failed to control its rapidly growing population: (1) policy targets were set very low; (2) central planning in highly decentralized federal states radically changed the outcome of family planning programs; (3) political parties in the central government were habitually opposed by political parties and factions that dominate state governments; (4) achieving a unified goal in population control policy was unlikely in India due to differing social and political realities in the federal states; (5) by the very nature of their existence, regional parties were dependent on the population size of their specific constituency and were more than reluctant to implement central government population control policies; and (6) the financial and man/woman power capabilities of governmental institutions, as well as their moral standing, were insufficient to complete the near-impossible task of changing the reproductive habits of a highly illiterate population (2002).

Consequently, while a commonly shared ideology glues society together, China's social structure institutionalizes the ideology of Chinese society. When the Chinese government decided to tighten its population control in the 1970s, China's family planning programs became effective right away, and its birth rate and natural increase rate continued to drop. However, when Indira Gandhi enforced the family planning program in India in 1976, it became the focus of attack by opposition parties during the elections in March 1977. With the defeat of the ruling party, the widely feared backlash occurred, leading to a sharp decline in program performance between 1977 and 1978 (Visaria and Jain, 1982).

Professor Srinivasan has also clearly pointed out such differences between China and India:

> while a country like China with one-party communist rule can impose on its people a stringent family size norm of one child per couple, and achieve considerable success without much popular revolt, India has not realized even the moderate fertility goals postulated in any of its first seven five-year plans.
>
> (Srinivasan, 2018: 20)

To implement population control policies, both China and India have established relevant organizations at different levels of the government; however, the results are different. In China, family planning offices are supported by different levels of the government. In India, however, the family planning centers are often not supported by the local governments. In China, the cadres who work in grassroots-level family planning offices are normally from the local community, and they can effectively talk about family planning to the local community, for they and the people they talk to are from either the same neighborhood or the same village. But in India, those who are working in village-level family planning centers are not local people. When they talk about birth control to villagers, they are perceived as outsiders, and the effectiveness of their work is substantially reduced (Wang, 2018). Obviously, the two kinds of governance in China and India, based on different social cultures and political structures, have been functioning differently. As a result, they implemented their population control policies differently and brought about different population changes.

Summary and Discussions

This chapter explains how differences in fundamental social facts have affected population control and population changes in China and India. These factors include religion and tradition, traditional values related to population, ethnicity and language, social class, family, the social status and education of women, and the functioning of governance. Variations in these social factors result from the two nations' different historical developments and external influences.

The fundamental differences between China and India date back to what happened in China and India more than 2,000 years ago. When the Qin Dynasty unified China, including its languages, system of weights and measures, and social norms and behaviors, India's Maurya Empire did not really unify the Indian subcontinent. Similarly, the establishment of the PRC was the result of a fundamental revolution led by Mao Zedong and the Communist Party, which fundamentally changed Chinese society and established a strong central government. The Chinese revolutions before 1949 and the mass campaigns launched by the Chinese government after 1949 smashed the traditional political structure, fundamentally changed traditional values, restructured traditional economic systems, eradicated traditional bias against women, got rid of many social ills like prostitution and opium, and improved the education of its people.

In contrast to China, Indian Independence was obtained through a civil disobedience and non-cooperation movement led by Mahatma Gandhi, Jawaharlal Nehru, and other nationalist leaders. The new government had not only inherited the British government system but also accepted the members of the colonial ICSs and made them the members of the independent IAS (Guha, 2007). India's more mildly independent movement, which relied on a new constitution to effect social change, may have helped in a smooth power transition but would not allow more fundamental changes in Indian traditional society.

Although Independence enabled the new government to make social improvements, elite-led social change started mostly in the upper levels of government through legislation or new policies. They have not fundamentally changed widespread and deeply held religious values or the traditional caste system. India's lack of fundamental changes from the grassroots level has prevented Indian society from eradicating bad traditions, such as the caste system, and, therefore, it has prevented the fundamental improvement of society. Similarly, legislation and government policies have not fundamentally changed traditional biases against women and low-caste people, which will continue to hinder India's development.

Because of different social facts, the population control policies adopted, the implementation of the policies, and the population changes in China and India are different, although both countries have intentions of controlling their rapidly growing populations to enhance socioeconomic developments. The chapter has paid more attention to the differences although China and India have also possessed many similarities which are not the focus of this book. A comparison of differences should make these fundamental social factors stand out and easy to understand.

The factors being compared are the most fundamental social factors that mark the unique characteristics of Chinese society. For example, the lack of a dominant religion alongside the unique traditional values of Confucianism, strong interlocked values in the family and state, substantially improved status and education of women, a more than 2,000-year-old bureaucratic government system, and highly centralized authoritative government control all indicate China's unique characteristics. At the same time, these factors have changed dramatically as a result of more than a century of bloody fighting against foreign invasions and for revolution.

Since the economic reforms started in the later 1970s, China's economic development has sped up and the country has become much richer than ever before. However, social inequality that had been substantially eliminated between the 1950s and 1970s reappeared. During the past four decades, government corruption has reached a dangerous point. At the same time, many old traditions, such as discrimination against women, that had been eliminated between the 1950s and 1970s, have reappeared. New problems such as the commercialization of marriage have reappeared, too. When old traditions have been reduced, some good traditional values and moralities have also been lost.

Nevertheless, the Chinese seem determined to resume China's dominant position in the world with unyielding efforts. Understanding these unique characteristics of Chinese society and the fundamental changes in modern China may help us understand population control policies, policy implementations, and population changes there. At the same time, understanding these unique characteristics and changes may also help us understand China, including its past, present, and future.

Similarly, these factors are also most fundamental to Indian society. In his book on modern India, Ramachandra Guha has summarized the most fundamental social conflicts in the contemporary Indian society, and these conflicts mostly run along five axes. First, there is caste which is a principal identity for many Indians, defining whom they may marry, associate with, and fight against. Second, there is language. The constitution of India recognizes 22 languages as official. Naturally, national unity and linguistic diversity have not always been seen to be compatible, and Indians speaking one tongue have fought with Indians who speak another. The third is religion. Since faith is as fundamental a feature of human identity as language, Indians worshipping one kind of God have sometimes quarreled with Indians worshipping another. The fourth is social class. India is a land of enormous social disparity. Indian entrepreneurs are fabulously wealthy while about 300 million individuals are living below the official poverty line. These axes of conflict operate both singly and in combination. Perhaps a fifth should be added and that is gender. When landless laborers are paid meager wages, the women among them are the lowest of all. When low castes face a social stigma, women among them suffer most of all. The holy men of each religion tend to assign their women an inferior position in this world and the next. As an axis of discrimination, gender is even more pervasive than others (Guha, 2007).

In fact, these conflicts were formed by India's historical and socioeconomic developments and have worked together to determine or affect the population control policies, policy implementations, and population changes in the past seven decades. A fundamental difference between China and India is that China experienced many fundamental changes in the past century and these changes have substantially reduced the traditional values and culture that could affect the population control policies, policy implementations, and socioeconomic development. Contrary to China, the diversified religions, the traditional values, the social inequality and the caste system, the unequal status of women, the divisive social structure, and disparate languages, all have not experienced sufficient changes that may enhance the population control and the development of Indian society.

When the Republic of India obtained its independence in 1947, first-generation leaders such as Jawaharlal Nehru and Vallabhbhai Patel were ambitious about India's development. They realized India had an overpopulation problem and adopted policies to control population growth earlier than did Chinese first-generation leaders. However, changes in the social factors that they could affect did not meet their expectations. Without fundamental changes in these social facts, India's development would sooner or later be hindered.

Comparatively speaking, the Chinese have attached a strong value to the family and the state while Indians have placed substantial value on their religions. National unity is cherished more by the Chinese and diversity is a phenomenon natural to Indians. Equality has been sought throughout Chinese history, and inequality seems more acceptable in Indian society. While the Chinese used to look for or work on a better life in this lifetime, many Indians used to expect a better life next time. Accordingly, Chinese are more material-oriented while Indians are more spiritual. The Chinese are more likely to rise up to fight for equality while the Indians are more tolerant of inequality. In the long run, each of these social characteristics may have its positive and negative impacts on China and India. But at present, they are more conducive to population controls in China than in India. Similarly, they are also more conducive to the socioeconomic development in China than in India.

Nevertheless, how current population changes affect the future of China and India still needs to be understood. China's quick reduction of its birth rate may be more conducive to the socioeconomic development at present but may also have negative consequences in the future. Similarly, India's slow or more natural reduction of birth rate may hinder India's current socioeconomic development but may also benefit Indian society positively in the long run.

At present, both China and India need further improvement in social equality, women's status, and the functioning of government organizations. For China, current high levels of social inequality, the commercialization of marriage, and the lowered moral standard may seriously affect the country's healthy development and will need particular attention from Chinese society. For India, to get rid of the caste system, further improve women's status and education, reduce social disparity, solidify the unity of India, and improve government effectiveness may decide to what extent the Indian society can develop in the future.

When India obtained its independence in 1947 and when the People's Republic of China was established in 1949, they adopted different political systems but carried out similar economic developmental strategies. Both perceived their huge and rapidly increasing population as an obstacle in their development. Their different political systems and developmental strategies were determined by their historical developments and socioeconomic conditions. Any wish to have done it differently would be only wishful, for their social realities are the most fundamental and determining factors. Based on population control policies, policy implementations, and population changes in China and India, it might be reasonable to say that China should have had a more democratic and less aggressive policy and India should have a more effective policy and more effective implementation, but their objective social realities are more decisive and have a stronger power to determine how things can be done. Of course, this does not mean that either the Chinese or the Indians should give up their subjective efforts to make things better.

References

Algu, Savannah. 2021. "Exploitation of Dowries in India". *Borgen Magazine*, November 29. Retrieved from www.borgenmagazine.com/dowries-in-india/.

Aspalter, C. 2002. "Population Policy in India". *The International Journal of Sociology and Social Policy* 22 (11–12): 48–72.

Choudhry, Misbah T. and J. Paul Elhorst. 2010. "Demographic Transition and Economic Growth in China, India and Pakistan". *Economic Systems* 34(3): 218–236.

CIA. 2017. "India, The World Factbook". Retrieved on October 6, 2017 from www.cia.gov/library/publications/the-world-factbook/geos/in.html.

CIA. 2020. "India, World Factbook". Retrieved on July 28, 2020 from https://theodora.com/wfbcurrent/india/india_people.html.

CIA. 2022a. "Religions, People and Society, China". *The World Factbook*. Retrieved from www.cia.gov/the-world-factbook/countries/china/summaries/#introduction.

CIA. 2022b. "Religions, People and Society, India". *The World Factbook*. Retrieved on July 21, 2022 from www.cia.gov/the-world-factbook/countries/india/#introduction.

Crabtree, Steve and Anita Pugliese. 2012. "China Outpaces India for Women in the Workforce: One in Six College-educated Indian Women Works Full Time for an Employer". *News Gallup*, November 2. Retrieved from https://news.gallup.com/poll/158501/china-outpaces-india-women-workforce.aspx.

Das, Gurcharan. 2002. *India Unbound: From Independence to the Global Information Age*. New Delhi: Penguin Books.

Di, Yang. 2019. "China Marks Highest Rate of Women in National Congress, Improvement Needed to Promote Engagement". *CGTN*, March 8. Retrieved from https://news.cgtn.com/news/3d3d674d78456a4d33457a6333566d54/index.html.

Dube, S. C. 1963. "Men's and Women's Roles in India: A Sociological Review", in Barbara E. Ward (ed.) *Women in the New Asia*. New York, NY: UN Educational Scientific and Cultural Organizations,190.

East-West Center. 2002. *Easter-West Research Program, Population and Health Studies, the Future of Population in Asia*. Honolulu, HI: Publication Sales Office.

Eggleston, Karen. 2016. *Policy Challenges From Demographic Change in China and India*. Stanford, CA: Shorenstein Asia-Pacific Research Center.

Embree, Ainslie T. 1972. *India's Search for National Identity*. New York, NY: Alfred A. Knopf.

Encyclopedia Britannica. 1978. *Encyclopedia Britannica*. Chicago: Encyclopedia Britannica, Inc.

Family. 1985. "The Transition from Extended Family to Nuclear Family". *People's Daily*, March 31, p. 8.

Fan, Suiqiong, Yue Qian and Alissa Koski. 2022. "Child Marriage in Mainland China". *Studies in Family Planning* 53(1): 23–42.
Gao, Yenqiang and Limo Lei. 1985. "Population Growth and Population Theory", in *An Introduction to Population Studies*. Hebei: Hebei People's Press.
Glinska, Gosia. 2020. "Entrepreneurship in China: The Rise of Female Billionaires". *UVA Darden: Ideas to Action*, May 27. Retrieved from https://ideas.darden.virginia.edu/entrepreneurship-in-china-the-rise-of-female-billionaires.
Golley, Jane and Rod Tyers. 2013. "Contrasting Giants: Demographic Change and Economic Performance in China and India". *Procedia: Social and Behavioral Sciences* 77: 353–383.
Guha, Ramachandra. 2007. *India after Gandhi: The History of the World's Largest Democracy*. New York, NY: Ecco, Imprint of Harper Collins Publishers.
Index Mundi. 2022. "India – Proportion of Seats by Women in National Parliaments (%)". Retrieved from www.indexmundi.com/facts/india/indicator/SG.GEN.PARL.ZS#:~:text=Proportion%20of%20seats%20held%20by%20women%20in%20national,a%20single%20or%20lower%20chamber%20held%20by%20women.
Jaspers, Karl. 1957. *"Confucius". Socrates Buddha Confucius Jesus-From the Great Philosophers*, Vol. I. New York: Harcourt, Brace & World, Inc.
Johnson, Kay Ann. 1983. "Introduction", in *Women, the Family and Peasant Revolution in China*. Chicago, IL: University of Chicago Press.
Jones, Gavin W. and Pravin Visaria. 1998. *Urbanization in Large Developing Countries: China, Indonesia, Brazil, and India* (International Studies in Demography). Oxford: Clarendon Press.
Kapur, Radhika. 2019. "Status of Women in Ancient India". *ResearchGate*, January. Retrieved from www.researchgate.net/publication/330220793_Status_of_Women_in_Ancient_India.
Khemundu, Kapila. 2019. "Changing Values in Contemporary Indian Society". *International Journal of Scientific and Research Publications*9 (9): 473–476.
Khilnani, Sunil. 1997. *The Idea of India*. New Delhi: Penguin Books.
Liu, Haiyen and Jingyuan Liu. 2010. "A Comparison of the Family Planning Policies in India and China". *South Asian Studies Quarterly* 4: 86–90.
Liu, Kewan. 2019. "How India Lost to China". *Zhihu*. Retrieved on July 10, 2022 from www.zhihu.com/question/363016870#wechat_redirect.
Livi-Bacci, Massimo. 2012. *A Concise History of World Population*, 5th Edition. West Sussex: Wiley-Blackwell.
Ma, A. and R. C. Zha. 1984. *A Preliminary Analysis of the Present Situation of China's Population*. Beijing: A Census of One Billion People, Population Census Office Under the State Council, Department of Population Statistics of the State Statistical Bureau (in Chinese).
Ma, Li. 2016. "Female Labor Force Participation and Second Birth Rates in South Korea". *Journal of Population Research*33 (2): 173–195.
Mahla, Pamal. 2021. "Woman in the Post-Independence India". *The Armchair Journal*. Retrieved on July 31, 2022 from https://armchairjournal.com/women-in-post-independence-india/.
Mandelbaum, David. 1970. *Society in India*. Berkeley, CA: University of California.
Mandelbaum, David. 1974. *Human Fertility in India*. Berkeley, CA: University of California.
Ortiz-Ospina, Esteban, Sandra Tzvetkova, and Max Roser. 2022. "Women's Employment". *Our World in Data*. Retrieved on July 29, 2022 from https://ourworldindata.org/female-labor-supply#summary.
Parsons, T. 1959. "Foreword", in C. K. Yang (ed.) *The Chinese Family in the Communist Revolution*. Cambridge, MA: The Technology Press, MIT.
Ranjan, Alok. 1999. *Population and Development: The Indian Perspective*. Datia: Shyam Institute.

San, Huipong. 2007. *The Cultural History of India*. Guiling: Guangxi Teacher's University.

Shrinivasan, Rukmini. 2012. "Working Women: India vs. China". *India Blogs, The Times of India*, November 6. Retrieved from https://blogs.timesofindia.indiatimes.com/development dialogue/working-women-india-v-china/.

Srinivasan, Krishnamurthy. 2017. *Population Concerns in India: Shifting Trends, Policies, and Programs*. New Delhi: Sage Publications India Pvt Ltd.

Srinivasan, Sharada and Shuzhuo Li. 2018. *Scarce Women and Surplus Men in China and India: Macro Demographics Versus Local Dynamics* (Demographic Transformation and Socio-Economic Development (8)). Cham: Springer.

Stolc, Phyllis E. W. 2008. "Seeking Zero Growth: Population Policy in China and India". *Graduate Journal of Asia-Pacific Studies* 6 (2): 10–32.

Strachey, John. 1988. *India*. London: Kegan, Paul, Trench.

Szczepanski, Kallie. 2020. "History of India's Caste System". *ThoughtCo*. Retrieved on December 9, 2022 from www.thoughtco.com/history-of-indias-caste-system-195496#:~:text=When%20the%20British%20Raj%20began%20to%20take%20power,that%20had%20been%20repealed%20by%20the%20Muslim%20rulers.

Tan, Chung, 2007. " 'Chindia'. Civilizational Interfacial Strength for the fortification of Chinese 'Superdome' Paradigm", in Tan Chung, Liu Zhaohua and Huang Rong (eds) *Chindia – Idealism and Realization*. Yun Chung: Ningxia People's Press.

United Nations Department of Economic and Social Affairs. 2022. *World Population to Reach 8 Billion on 15 November 2022*. Retrieved on March 20, 2023 from https://www.un.org/en/desa/world-population-reach-8-billion-15-november-2022.

United Nations Development Programme (UNDP). 2022. "The 2020 Human Development Report". Retrieved from www.un.org/development/desa/pd/sites/www.un.org.development.desa.pd/files/undesa_pd_2022_global_population_growth.pdf.

Visaria, Pravin and Anruth K. Jain. 1982. "India", in *International Encyclopedia of Population*. New York, NY: Macmillan and the Free Press.

Wang, Gabe T. 1999. *China's Population: Problems, Thoughts and Policies*. Aldershot: Ashgate Publishing Limited.

Wang, Gabe T. 2018. "A Comparison of the Population Changes and the Social Factors That Affected the Changes". *Jiang Su Social Sciences* 2018 (5): 82–91.

Wu, C. P. 1986. "Theoretical Explanation on Rapid Decline of China's Fertility". *Population Research*1: 10–16.

Wu, Xing. 2002. "India, a Closed Democratic Country". *Hua Xia Wen Zhai Express*, April 8. Retrieved from http://www.cnd.org/HXWZ/CM02/cm0204a.gb.html.

Xia, Yan R. and Zhou Zhi G. 2003. "The Transition of Courtship, Mate Selection, and Marriage in China", in *Mate Selection across Cultures*. Thousand Oaks, CA: SAGE, 231–246.

You, Longyi. 2007. " 'Chindia' Theoretical Bases", in Tan Chung, Liu Zhaohua and Huang Rong (eds) *Chindia – Idealism and Realization*. Yun Chung: Ningxia People's Press.

Zeng, Benxiang. 2014. "Women's Political Participation in China: Improved or Not?" *Journal of International Women's Studies*15 (1): 136–150.

Zuckerman, Arthur. 2020. "56 Marriage Statistics: 2020/2021 Global Data, Analysis & Trends". *CompareCamp*, May 31. Retrieved from CompareCamp.com.

7 China, India, and the World

Summary and Discussions

The Population Control Policies and Implementations in China and India

In the past century, many scholars and political figures have perceived population explosions as one of the most fundamental challenges to the world. Many countries have risen to the challenge and adopted population control policies to reduce population growth. Among those nations, the population control policies adopted and implemented by China and India, the two most populous nations with about 37% of the world's total population in 1970, seem most important. Since population control policies are also important to socioeconomic development, the implementation of population control policies in China and India was expected to influence socioeconomic development substantially.

However, population control policy adoption, policy implementation, and population change cannot be fully understood as a population issue, for they are closely related to many aspects of the society. A nation's population, including the size, change, and quality, is the most fundamental issue of the society. Without fully understanding the population, we cannot fully understand the society. Similarly, without adequately understanding the society, we cannot fully understand the population issue. Therefore, this book has attempted to understand population control policies and policy implementations in China and India through traditional culture, religion, social structure, government effectiveness, and women's status. At the same time, it has taken a comparative approach. As an old Chinese saying advises that it does not matter if you do not understand something, a comparison will show you the truth.

During the 1950s and 1960s, both India and China perceived their enormous and rapidly growing population as an obstacle to their badly needed socioeconomic development. Therefore, both governments advocated for population control as an important developmental strategy, and both adopted and implemented restrictive population control policies. Now, seven decades after the Indian government-initiated population controls and five decades after the Chinese government began its nationwide population control, China's population growth has been more effectively controlled, and its economy has developed more rapidly than India's

DOI: 10.4324/9781003307419-7

although both nations' population growth rates have fallen, and both economies have been developing rapidly.

Between 1950 and 2020, India's population has grown more rapidly than China's. As a result, India's percentage of China's population increased from about 69.2% in 1950 to about 99.0% in 2020. In fact, India will overtake China to become the most populous nation in the world in 2023 (United Nations Department of Economic and Social Affairs, 2022a). In contrast to its population growth, China's economy has developed more rapidly than India's between 1950 and 2022. Per capita GDP was about $614 in China and about $597 in India in 1950 (NationMaster, 2022). In 2020, per capita GDP was $10,580.00 for China and $1,880.00 for India (IMF, 2021). From 1950 to 2020, India's per capita GDP declined from about 97% to about 18% of China's. Obviously, China's population control policies have been implemented much more effectively than India's. At the same time, China's economy has been developed more rapidly than India's.

Differences in population control policies, policy implementations, population changes, and socioeconomic developments between China and India are the result of different developments, exogenous impacts, religion and traditional values, perspectives on population, social structures, family roles, the status and education of women, and government functional effectiveness.

Naturally, the differences between the two nations today will make a difference in the future. China and India will have different population problems in the days to come. While India continues to face overpopulation problems, China will have to deal with the problems brought about by its population decline, such as rapid aging in the coming decades and an imbalanced sex structure. While the Chinese may enjoy a higher per capita GDP, India may have a younger and more dynamic labor force. While Indian society may still be hampered by its traditions, such as the unequal status of women and the caste system, Chinese society may suffer from its substantially reduced traditions, such as strong family values and traditional moralities.

Now, it is too soon to make a historical evaluation of the population control policies that have been adopted and implemented in China and India. Population changes in the two societies will have long-term consequences. According to the experience of other developed nations, when birth rates decrease below the replacement level, it is difficult to reverse the trend. China may have to worry about low birth rates in the future.

> On the other hand, India's sustained population growth has probably been an obstacle to the modernization of the country and worsened many social problems, although it has not impeded the acceleration of economic growth and may spare the country the shock of violent changes in the age structure.
>
> (Livi-Bacci, 2012: 194)

Which of the two countries has taken a better course? The question may be better answered by future considerations of economic and sustainable development, as well as demographic and social factors in the two nations.

The more rapid urbanization in China than in India has also contributed to different population trajectories in the two nations. In 1960, the urbanization rate was 19.8% in China and 17.9% in India. However, in 2019, it was 62.7% in China and 34.5% in India (see Table 2.1 and Table 3.1). The different urbanization rates not only reflect different socioeconomic development but also contribute to population changes in the two nations. According to Bricker and Ibbitson (2019), the most fundamental factor that affects the birth rate is urbanization. When people move into cities, children become a liability instead of an asset. Educated women in the urban areas prefer autonomy over having many children. Programs that provide child support and parental leave may not alter the situation. This fundamental change in the world's population will restructure societies in surprising and destabilizing ways. With fewer young people working and consuming, the demand-driving economies will stagnate. Therefore, China's rapid reduction of its population growth may also be attributed to its rapid socioeconomic development and urbanization as well as effective population control policies.

On the other hand, India's population growth has also slowed down in the past few decades, which may be attributed less to its population control policies but more to its socioeconomic development. Therefore, India's overpopulation problem may be more effectively solved by socioeconomic development and urbanization. When people live in urban areas, the need to have many children will be reduced and the need to get education will be increased. The well-known statement that economic development is society's best contraceptive is probably true, especially in India. Many of the problems based on the old religious traditions, such as child marriage and discrimination of women, may be easier to reduce in urban areas. Similarly, when people move to urban areas, the impact of the caste system can be reduced more easily.

Today, when comparing and evaluating population control policies in China and India, it is reasonable to point out that if China had continued to implement a two-children-per-couple policy (or the later marriage, longer intervals between two children, and fewer children per family policy implemented in the 1970s) between 1980 and 2015 instead of the highly controversial one-birth-per-couple policy, China's population growth would not be much different from the one-birth-per-couple policy, given rapid socioeconomic development and urbanization. It might have taken a little longer to lower birth and population increase rates, but negative impacts on the family, deeply held family values, a balanced structure of the two sexes, and an aging society, could have been much smaller. At the same time, the implementation of the two-child policy could be much easier and cost the government much less financially and politically.

On the other hand, if India had adopted a two-child policy, or if its population control policies had been aimed at limiting the number of children for each family instead of focusing on the number of sterilizations, India's population control could have been more effective, which may have enhanced India's socioeconomic development. At the same time, if Indian society had conferred on women higher status, better education, and had broken the caste system as the government intended, India's population control could have been more effective and economic development more rapid.

China's and India's Population Issues in a World Perspective

During the 18th century, China's population increased substantially, partially due to the Qing government's efforts in developing agriculture and increasing population. As a result, Chinese scholars, such as Hong Liangji (1746–1806) began to worry about the rapid population increase and its negative impact on socioeconomic development in China. In his essay *On Governance and Well-being of the Empire*, published in 1793, Hong noted that China's population increased fivefold in 30 years, tenfold in 60 years, and 20-fold in a 100 years while tillable land and food supply were limited. There was a problem when a house for one person had to be shared by ten or 100, or when the food for one person had to be shared by ten or 100 people. Therefore, Hong, greatly concerned about the rapidly increasing population, warned the government about the dire consequence of the explosive population increase and made specific suggestions to control population growth in China (Hong, 1793). Although Hong's warning of overpopulation in China appeared even earlier than Thomas Robert Malthus's tract on England, he did not make much influence of China or the world.

Then, it was Malthus's 1798 *An Essay on the Principle of Population* that got the world's attention. Malthus, a true believer that population growth needed to be controlled and people should have family planning, planned his family rationally, waiting until he was 39 to marry and have children. He had only three children (Weeks, 2016). Later, the Malthusian perspective became widely shared, and rapid population growth became a world concern.

As the world's population changed, dominant Western views on population size and economic growth changed as well. During the 1920s, the dominant perspective was to worry about overpopulation. During the 1930s, the prevailing view was to worry about underpopulation. During the 1950s and 1960s, the most prominent perspective was to worry about a population explosion when the world's population was growing more and more rapidly. As a result, world's population control policies, especially in the developing nations, were intensely promoted.

The world's population increased rapidly during the 20th century from 1.65 billion in 1900 to 6.13 billion in 2000. Then, it further increased to eight billion in 2022. Population increases, however, have varied across the world. Most of the increase in population during the 20th century occurred in developing countries in Africa, Asia, and Latin America. Within a century, Africa's percentage of the world's population increased from 8.1% to 13%, Asia's percentage increased from 57% to 62%, and Latin America's increased from 4.5% to 8.5% while Europe's share decreased from 24.7% to 11.2%. The major reason behind these dramatic changes is the improvements in agriculture and health care, both of which enabled the world to feed more people and people to live longer. Although the Industrial Revolution promoted population increase during the 18th century, it was increased food production, peace, and relatively stable development after Second World War that promoted rapid increases in population in developing nations.

As a result, the overpopulation problem morphed into a concern about population growth in developing countries during the 20th century. This concern reached its peak in the1970s when world's population growth rates reached their highest points. Scholars and political figures in Western nations worried about population growth in developing or newly independent nations after the Second World War and strongly promoted population controls in these nations. The population of developing nations grew explosively during the second half of the 20th century and fueled concern about the world's limited resources. The US government even considered population growth in developing nations as an issue of US national security and its overseas interests (Clowes, 2020).

Under these circumstances, India began its population limitation program in the early 1950s. The program gradually developed into more restrictive population control programs in the 1970s. Tens of millions of dollars in loans from the World Bank, the Swedish International Development Authority, and the United Nations Population Fund encouraged the Indian government's large-scale sterilization efforts. The efforts reached their peak in 1975 when the Indian prime minister suspended civil liberties and sterilized over six million people in a single year (Follett, 2019). Increasingly tightened population control was derailed; however, by the 1977 election. Ironically, population control relaxed when world's population growth reached its most rapid period.

Although China's nationwide population control actually started in the early 1970s, after the PRC joined the United Nations in 1971 and started to open its door to the Western world, it was also influenced by Western perspectives. In 1979, China instituted its one-birth-per-couple policy, inspired by The Limits to Growth (Follett, 2019). In fact, population controls in both India and China were strongly encouraged and financially supported by Western nations, often through the United Nations. Since the Chinese government is more powerful and has had stable control of the nation, China's population control has been more restrictive, persistent, and effective than India's.

However, while some scholars and governments worried about overpopulation problems, others started to worry about underpopulation. For example, in their book, *Empty Planet: The Shock of Global Population Decline*, Darrell Bricker and John Ibbitson (2019) predicted that the world's population would peak about eight or nine billion around the middle of this century and start to decline to about seven billion by the end of the century. Currently, populations are declining in many developed nations. China has been the most populous nation in the world, but its birth rate has been below the replacement level since the 1990s. Even India's birth rate level is approaching the replacement level.

India relaxed its population control policies in 1977, which coincided with a gradual slowing of world's population growth. However, it was too early for India for its population was still huge, and its growth was continuing apace. On the other hand, China's policy adjusted to two children per couple in 2015 and three children per couple in 2021seems a little bit later than it should be, for China's birth rate has been below the replacement level since the 1990s and a stable population could be more conducive to China's socioeconomic development.

In today's world, overpopulation is mostly perceived as a developing countries' problem, and population control policies are generally thought to be the province of less developed nations. While most less developed countries want to control their population growth to allow socioeconomic development, developed nations need to encourage population growth to maintain stable socioeconomic development. In the more developed regions in the world, nearly 50% of governments had policies to increase their population growths while only 2% had policies to decrease population growth in 2013. In contrast to more developed regions, nearly half of the governments in less developed regions had policies to decrease their population growth while only 10% had policies to increase population growth. Between 2010 and 2015, among the 18 countries with negative population growth, 16 had policies to increase population growth (United Nations Department of Economic and Social Affairs, 2017).

By 2019, 69 governments had policies to lower fertility, 55 government had policies aimed to raise fertility, and 19 government had policies focused on maintaining current levels of fertility. At the same time, 54 governments had no fertility population control policy. While a long-term trend in fertility decline will lead to increased population aging and smaller populations in many countries, to reverse long-term downward trends in fertility has proven more difficult to achieve than lowering fertility rates (United Nations Department of Economic and Social Affairs, 2022b). Obviously, rapid population increase is not a world phenomenon, and population controls are not desperately needed for the whole world today.

More important, the development of the world and the growth of the human population seem to indicate that the much-feared population explosion might be only for a short period of human history. So far, world's population growth and economic development have definitely shown that Malthus's perspective that population growth will outrun economic development was wrong. During the 20th century, world's population increased fourfold from about 1.65 billion to about 6.13 billion while the world's economy increased about 16 times from about $1,500 billion at the beginning of the century to $24,000 billion by the end of the century. More obviously, during the second half of the century, birth rates have substantially declined in almost all countries. Between 1960 and 2006, the world's per capita GDP increased 2.4 times while the average birth rate reduced from 5.4 percent in 1962 to 2.5 percent in 2006 (China Development Research Foundation, 2012).

> The growth rate of the world's population peaked in 1965–1970, when it was increasing by 2.1 per cent per year, on average. Since then, the pace of global population growth has slowed by half, falling below 1.1 per cent per year in 2015–2020, and it is projected to continue to slow through the end of this century.
>
> (United Nations Department of Economic and Social Affairs, 2019: 5)

On the other hand, the United Nations Department of Economic and Social Affairs (2022a) also reported that the world's population has more than tripled since the middle of the 20th century, rising from around 2.5 billion in 1950 to about eight billion in 2022. Therefore, rapid population growth is still a common feature of the demographic transition at present, and most of the world's future population growth will take place in developing countries. While the population in many developing nations will continue to grow rapidly, especially in Africa, population growth in China has already stabilized, and the population of India will also gradually stabilize. The population control in China has contributed to the stabilization of the world's population growth while India's population growth still contributes to the growth of the world's population. The greatest concern about population growth during the next few decades may remain mostly in Africa.

When talking about different perspectives on population and development, we cannot confine our thinking only to Malthus's mode of thinking and limit our attention to the increase or decrease in population numbers. Instead, we should also look into the positive side of population increase and consider people as producers. At the same time, we should also think that the development of science and technology can be unlimited. Furedi (1997) has summarized eight perspectives in his book which may also give us some alternative ideas about the contradictions between population and development. Although traditional Malthusian concerns assumed that population growth may have a negative and potentially destructive impact on the environment, socioeconomic development may not only reduce family size or population growth but also provide solutions to the shortage of natural resources. At the same time, environmental problems may also be solved through scientific and technological developments. However, human society's efforts in social justice may better distribute wealth and resources, and reduce the poverty caused by overpopulation. More important, as Mao has pointed out, people are the most precious things in the world. If human societies are well-managed and human resources are well utilized, the world may not have to worry much about the overpopulation issue.

When we think about population control policies in China and India from a world's population perspective, it is reasonable to suggest that China lifts its population controls now while its birth rate has already been below the replacement level. India's population is still growing rapidly and may need population control policies for more years. Along with its dynamic economic development and slow but continuous social improvement, Indian population growth will gradually stabilize.

For China and India, a large but stabilized population may be more conducive to socioeconomic development in the 21st century. Government efforts in population control in these two nations should also be directed at improving the quality rather than the quantity of their populations. Besides population control policies, social equality, gender equality, better education, and better quality of life are also fundamental to the life of all the people in China and India.

Population Growth and Socioeconomic Development in China and India

In human history, population can be seen as a crude index of prosperity. During the Paleolithic Age, the world had a million inhabitants. During the Neolithic Age, the world had ten million people. Then, during the Bronze Age, the world had about 100 million people. When the world experienced the Industrial Revolution, it had a billion people (Livi-Bacci, 2012). At present, world's population has reached about eight billion. By the end of the 21st century, the world may have ten billion people. Generally speaking, population is the most fundamental power of the world development, and population growth is also a result of world development. The huge populations in China and India today are the result of their great socioeconomic developments in the past, and they are also the most fundamental factor in their future socioeconomic development.

After the Second World War, many developing countries tried to control population growth to promote socioeconomic development. Among all the developing countries, China and India seem quite successful in their socioeconomic development. Within the next two decades, China and India are projected to be the first and the third largest economies in the world. One of the important reasons for China's and India's success is that their huge populations consist of not only a huge number of consumers but also a great number of producers in the world market.

According to population growth and economic development in China and India, population and economic development were mutually correlated for the past 40 years. Population growth itself may promote economic development. However, rapid population growth in today's world may slow down economic development. On the other hand, slowing down population growth may accelerate economic development. To increase per capita GDP and improve individual lives, rapid population growth needs to be controlled. When a large percentage of the population moves into urban areas, economic development may stagnate or even reduce population growth because urban residents holding dominant world values, such as individualism, are not conducive to family and population growth.

In a specific society, when sufficient capital and natural resources are available for the existing population, the population growth can be a positive factor for a rapid economic development. On the other hand, when neither sufficient capital nor natural resources are available, a rapidly increasing population may negatively affect economic development, and society may have an overpopulation problem. In contrast, when capital and natural resources are available but there is an insufficient labor supply, a problem of underpopulation may call for a policy to encourage more rapid population growth. In the world today, few societies have a perfect match between population and available capital and natural resources. Each society may need to either reduce or increase its population to develop its economy.

Of course, whether a society can fully utilize its human resources for its economic development depends on social justice and human development. If a society allows and enables a higher percentage of the population to participate in economic activities, its population is more likely to become producers rather than consumers. Social equality, including gender equality, allows a higher percentage of the population to participate in economic activities. At the same time, the quality of the population is also important. Education can improve population quality and allows a larger portion of the labor force to become effective. In both areas, China's social condition seems better than India's, a fundamental reason why China's socioeconomic development has increased more than India's.

However, it still needs to be seen how much population control policies will affect economic development. China's reduced population growth may enable the country to invest more and to increase the labor productivity to promote its economic development. On the other hand, India's continuous population growth will provide the nation with a larger labor force, enhancing economic development.

China and India's Population Issue in a Historical Perspective

This book has focused much of its attention on population control policy differences between China and India; however, when taking everything into consideration, China and India have multiple similarities. Both have huge populations because their agriculture and health care have developed over their long history, evidence of past successful accomplishments.

In their long history, both were pro-nature and attempted to live cohesively with nature. Similarly, both attached great importance to harmonious relationships among their people and respected different religious beliefs. Although Chinese society was mostly non-religious, both societies were polytheistic, and different religions existed side by side peacefully most of the time in history. While Indians relied mostly on religions and religious tolerance as a basis for social stability, the Chinese utilized tradition to establish highly stable societies. Their effective governance or little governance has not only created and accumulated substantial wealth but also supported enormous populations. During 18 of the last 20 centuries, China and India were the largest economies in the world (Maddison, 2008) and the two largest populations. Before the Industrial Revolution, socioeconomic development and population were closely related, and large populations normally developed large economies and only large economies could support large populations.

However, stable societies like China and India were vulnerable while facing the external invasions of the Western nations who shared neither their traditions nor their religions. The Indian defeat at Plassey in 1757 and the British defeat of China less than a century later during the First Opium War in 1840 brought serious damage to the two great civilizations. Most important, their economies were destroyed. During 1700, China's economy was 23.1% and India's economy was 22.6% of the world's total economy. In 1820, China's economy further increased to 32.4% while the Indian economy was reduced to 15.7% of the world's total economy. Since then, the economies of China and India initially declined. And similarly, their population growth also slowed down. Between 1840 and 1930, China's population only increased from 412 million in 1840 to 489 million in 1930 (Wang, 1999).

Within 90 years, China's population only increased 19% and the yearly average increase rate was only 0.2%. Similarly, India's total population increased from only 169 million in 1800 to 376 million in 1950 (Statista, 2022). Within 150 years, India's total population increased only 122%, and the average annual increase rate was only 0.8%.

However, their defeat by Western powers also marked the beginning of the rebirth of the two largest nations in the world. Although stability was upset, peace was destroyed, and the economy was ruined in China and India, nationalism was awakened and struggles for their independence also began. Eventually, Western invasions ushered in Western values, science, and technology, combined with their historical traditions. Although their economies as a share of the world's total economy fell to 5.2% for China and 3.4% for India in 1952 (Ramesh, 2005), both were ready to rise again after the establishment of their independent governments.

Why, despite huge populations and highly developed economies before the Industrial Revolution, did China and India fall behind Western nations? First, in their long history, their traditional cultures may have been too strongly established and therefore affected their development. For example, the Chinese scholars paid great attention mostly to the relationship between different groups of people in the society, and Indian scholars focused their attention on the relationship between human beings and gods or goddess, both of which were different from Western society's great attention to the relationship between human beings and nature. China attached great importance to traditional values and norms and gave too much respect to its ancestors, which prevented social and technological development. Similarly, India firmly stuck to its deeply held religious values and caste traditions, preventing social changes or social development. Therefore, Western culture might be more conducive to the development of science and technology.

Second, their advanced development of agriculture required China and India to have a stable society. With both possessing enormous populations, they could neglect developing new technology, instead relying readily on an abundant and hard-working labor force to develop its agricultural economy.

Third, when the British colonized India between the 19th and the first half of the 20th century, British control prevented the development of Indian society, despite bringing new technology to the Indian subcontinent. Similarly, between the middle of the 17th and the early 20th centuries, the Chinese were ruled by *Manchu*, a minority from Northern China. The Manchu minority's control of the majority Han population fundamentally prevented the development of Chinese society. As a result, Indians and Chinese were unable to develop their economy and society more effectively.

After many years of struggle, both countries obtained independence and reorganized their societies. In the past century, both nations have changed fundamentally. They know that in this capitalist-dominated world, they have to give up at least part of their traditional values or spiritual values, they must be strong, and they must develop their economy, science, and technology.

When they became independent nations, their enormous populations were perceived as burdensome to their socioeconomic development and both have adopted restrictive population control policies to curb the growth of their huge populations. Population control efforts were partly led by and fit into Western society's strong desire to control population growth in developing nations. Now, when population growth has been reduced or stabilized, their huge populations are more likely to become a great labor force or human resource that will enable them to develop their societies economically, scientifically, and socially. Just as their histories, religions, traditional values, and socioeconomic developments have shaped their current populations, their current populations will determine their future socioeconomic development. Both China and India have the potential to develop into the largest economies in the world again.

Another shared phenomenon is that many scholars and political figures in Western countries lack an accurate understanding of either China or India post-liberation/Independence in the late 1940s. Traditionally, India was an old civilization in many states. After its Independence in 1947, India became an old civilization within a young state. As Khilnani (1997) points out, the arrival of a modern state on the Indian landscape over the past century and a half and its growth and consolidation as a stable entity after 1947 are decisive historical facts that mark a shift from a society where authority was secured by diverse local methods to one where it is located in a single, sovereign agency. When the Republic of India was first established in 1947 and inherited its Western political system of democracy, many people, including political figures and scholars, doubted the vast nation would hold together—there were so many factors that suggested a disintegration of the newly formed republic. Now, more than seven decades later, socially divided India has not only remained a unified republic with its unique, seemingly less effective governance, but it also has become more dynamic in its socioeconomic development.

Similarly, when the PRC was first established in 1949, few people in the world had faith in the future development of the largest country in the world, and many Western nations did not like the Chinese government, either. China was an old civilization with a highly centralized government most of the time since the Qin Dynasty. The founding of the PRC reestablished its strong central government and sovereignty. Most scholars and political figures in Western nations did not like the fundamental changes that occurred in the Chinese society and strongly believed that China had taken the wrong path. After the Korean War in the early 1950s, Western countries actually blockaded China and would have liked to have seen the new Chinese government fail. Especially after the collapse of the former Soviet Union, many predicted the fall of the Chinese government many times. Nevertheless, China firmly carried out its reforms and continued its socioeconomic development. Instead of collapsing like the former Soviet Union, Chinese society continued its improvement even more quickly than most nations in the world. Within seven decades, China has changed from a weak, divided, chaotic, and poverty-stricken nation into a strong and highly unified country with highly dynamic socioeconomic development. Although China and India are different, the establishment of their independent governments has definitely indicated their dynamic socioeconomic developments and the rapid growth of their enormous populations.

Still another similarity between China and India is that when both new governments began in the late 1940s, they adopted similar economic development strategies. In China, Mao and the Communist government chose socialism as its economic development ideology and adopted some government mechanisms from the former Soviet Union. When India obtained its independence in 1947, Nehru wanted to adopt a capitalist political system and a socialist economy. Therefore, China took a socialist road, and India adopted a socialistic road. Both implemented five-year economic development plans.

More than seven decades after the establishment of the PRC, Chinese society has developed substantially, and China's economy has become the second largest economy in the world. Such an impressive achievement has been the result of land reform, getting rid of superstitious beliefs, substantial efforts to reduce illiteracy, fundamental improvements of women's status, enormous achievements in farmland construction, the construction of vast irrigation systems, and the establishment of the industrial systems between the 1950s and 1970s. Besides all these factors, China has successfully controlled the rapid growth of its huge population.

The Indian government adopted similar policies to promote its socioeconomic development. It carried out land reforms, improved women's status, adopted policies to improve the socioeconomic status of the lower castes, initiated a green revolution in rural areas, and considerably improved the education of its citizens. Even before China started its population controls, the Indian government adopted and implemented population controls. As a result, its economy has developed substantially. More than seven decades after its independence, the Indian economy became the fifth economy in the world in 2022. However, traditional social conditions that did not fundamentally change the caste system proved less successful in improving women's status and the compromised land reform substantially reduced the effective implementation of policies in India.

After three or four decades of practice, both the Chinese and Indian governments realized the need to reform their socioeconomic development strategies. China started its economic reforms during the late 1970s, and India started its reforms in the early 1990s; both intended to promote economic development, and both accomplished a great deal. Ever since the reforms started, both nations have given up some of the ideological values held by first-generation leaders and adopted market mechanisms in their economic development.

China's embracing of Western culture has substantially promoted its economic development but has also destroyed much of its already-weakened social morality. Excessive efforts at getting rich have created great social inequality, which threatens social stability if it is not appropriately controlled and controlled in time. At the same time, many years of social reforms and restrictive population control have seriously damaged its fundamental family values. However, after the 20th Communist Party Congress in 2022, the newly established leadership seems ready to handle the problems that emerged after reforms began in the late 1970s. As for the Indian society, its strong religious tradition has slowed down its economic development but may keep society stabilized despite that religious or ethnic conflict may continue to affect socioeconomic development.

Although their developments bumped along during the first few decades, China and India have gradually made appropriate adjustments and sped up their developments. Now, China and India are ready to rise again. By 2020, China's GDP became the world's second largest and India's the fifth. If calculated by purchasing power parity (which is the measurement of prices of specific goods to compare the absolute purchasing power parity in different country's currencies, and it allows for economists to compare economic productivity and standards of living between countries), China already had the largest and India had the third largest economy in 2015 (World Bank, 2022). Therefore, it is reasonable to expect China and India to become the largest and the second largest economies in the world.

The fourth similarity China and India share is that both had been great civilizations and now have the potential to rise again to be great nations in the world. Having eventually learned how to compete with Western nations with newly obtained knowledge and technology, they are now ready to rise again and destined to become dominant nations in the world. In the long history of their development, they have just been interrupted and forced to make some adjustments in their directions and strategies. Now, they will move on and remain great civilizations, as they were before. With strong traditional values that are pro-nature and pro-world humanity and harmony, these two civilizations may offer the world a new way of development and contribute to world peace and stability.

In the past, China has been one of the most advanced civilizations. Between 1840 and 1949, China fell behind the Western nations and was deeply humiliated and repeatedly abused. After more than a century of unyielding struggle and bloody fighting, China stood up again, as Mao declared on the Tiananmen Tower in 1949 when the People's Republic of China was established. With its unified language, highly shared ideology of national revival, a unified national power structure, a strong central government with a highly sophisticated bureaucratic system that has existed for more than 2,000 years, and a huge and hardworking population, China is determined to become a rich and strong nation in the world. China's socioeconomic development or its revival is unstoppable.

India has the second largest population and will become the most populous nation in the world in 2023. In the past 4,000 years, it has prospered for many centuries. However, since the British East Company obtained trading rights in 1617, its influence in India grew steadily as the Mughal empire was declining. After the India's defeat at Plassey in 1757, the East India Company took political control over a large part of India. Finally, the British Parliament placed India directly under the control of the British crown after the Sepoy Rebellion in 1857. Then, India was totally colonized by the British until its independence in 1947. After many years of hard struggle and noncooperation campaigns, started in the early 1920s under the leadership of Mahatma Gandhi, India eventually obtained its independence, which allowed the Indian subcontinent to become a unified country controlled by a central government. After more than seven decades of continuous development, India's total economy surpassed that of Britain and became the fifth largest economy in the world in 2022. Now, with its huge, young, and hardworking population, India is destined to rise again, and its socioeconomic development could be even more rapid in the days to come.

Both China and India are likely to resume their historical positions in the world and their economies will become the largest and the second largest in the world in the foreseeable future. With long histories and different cultures, both nations possess unique traditions, values, and strategies in their socioeconomic development, which other countries can learn from or at least understand. However, while both China and India are forging ahead, many people in the Western world seem satisfied with the little they know about the two most populous nations in the world. Worse still, many people are more and more reluctant to understand China.

Of course, China and India are also different from each other, and they are different from the rest of the world. India's long history and huge population formed its unique values, religions, and development strategies. India's highly diversified religious beliefs, diversified population, numerous languages, philosophical reasoning, and hardworking people are great characteristics of a society, all of which require a great deal of efforts to understand. India's population and social conditions seem to fit the political system which India partly inherited from the British.

China is even more unique. Its long tradition and huge population formed its unique values, philosophies, and development strategies all of which are often different from those of Western nations. For example, Chinese holistic thinking is different from Western societies' analytic thinking. Chinese dialectic analysis of things is different from Western society's dichotomous analysis of things. While the Chinese are trying to adopt whatever is useful from the Western societies, either scientific knowledge or market mechanisms, Western societies seem to expect the Chinese to copy only the Western political system and social values; seldom do they think that they may also learn something from the Chinese who have survived for more than 4,000 years and have 18% of the world's population.

China and India will develop rapidly but they will also develop differently. In China, its current social structure and political system are the result of its long historical traditions, unique cultural and social values, socioeconomic conditions, and humiliating history between 1840 and 1949. Many people in the Western nations believe that the Chinese government is authoritative and unfit to China, but seldom do they understand it was the unique social conditions, cultural values, and history that have shaped the current political system and government in China. China will develop rapidly and will develop in its unique ways.

In India, while religions, languages, cultures, castes, values, and social statuses are highly diversified, social communication, decision making by the government, or implementation of policies within India cannot be efficient. In such a society, a democratic political system fits the society quite well but ineffectiveness is almost guaranteed. If India tries to establish an authoritarian government or to be as assertive as China does, it may run into trouble or the risk of breaking up, for such an effort may run directly against its social conditions, as, for example, Indira Gandhi's attempt to control Indian population growth during the middle of the 1970s shows. As Desai has pointed out:

> India will remain a soft state, a consensual polity, and it will not be capable of sustained growth at the sort of rates which China has attained. To stay a stable

> peaceful society, India has to be a muddle and a mess. . . . India and China will both remove poverty in their midst and cease to be bywords for misery that they became for a hundred and fifty years after 1820. China will again become a viable Great Power; India may become just a Great Democracy.
> (Desai, 2003: 18)

During the middle of the 20th century, their enormous populations were perceived as their biggest burdens in their socioeconomic development. But now in the 21st century, their populations can be great resources for socioeconomic development. With their huge and hardworking populations, China and India are ready again to become great economies and great civilizations in the world.

References

Bricker, Darrell and John Ibbitson. 2019. *Empty Planet: The Shock of Global Population Decline*. New York: Broadway Books.

China Development Research Foundation. 2012. *Development Report of China 2011/12, Population Change and Adjustment of Population Policy*. Beijing: China Development Press.

Clowes, Brian. 2020. "National Security Study Memorandum 200: Blueprint for World Depopulation". *Human Life International: Empowering You to Build a Pro-life World*, July 17. Retrieved from www.hli.org/resources/nssm-200/.

Desai, Meghnad. 2003. "India and China: An Essay in Comparative Political Economy". Paper for the IMF Conference on India/China, Delhi, November.

Follett, Chelsea. 2019. "The Cruel Truth About Population Control". *The National Interest*, June 13. Retrieved from https://nationalinterest.org/feature/cruel-truth-about-population-control-62467.

Furedi, Frank. 1997. *Population & Development: A Critical Introduction*. New York, NY: St. Martin's Press.

Hong, Liangji. 1793. "On Governance and Well-being of the Empire". *The Classical Poems and Essays Website*. Retrieved on October, 12, 2022 from https://so.gushiwen.cn/shiwenv_5f2f57055288.aspx (Chinese language website).

IMF. 2021. "Data Mapper, Real GDP Growth: Annual Percentage Change, 1980–2025". Retrieved on March 26, 2021 from www.imf.org/external/datamapper/NGDP_RPCH@WEO/OEMDC/ADVEC/WEOWORLD/CHN.

Khilnani, Sunil. 1997. *The Idea of India*. New Delhi: Penguin Books.

Livi-Bacci, Massimo. 2012. *A Concise History of World Population*, 5th Edition. Malden, MA: John Wiley and Sons, Ltd.

Maddison, Angus. 2008. "Angus Maddison Statistics of the Ten Largest Economies by GDO (PPP). WikipediA: The Free Encyclopedia". Retrieved on March 20, 2023 from https://en.wikipedia.org/wiki/Angus_Maddison_statistics_of_the_ten_largest_economies_by_GDP_(PPP).

NationMaster. 2022. "Economy>GDP Per Capita in 1950: Countries Compared". Retrieved on September 4, 2022 from www.nationmaster.com/country-info/stats/Economy/GDP-per-capita-in-1950.

Ramesh, Jairam. 2005. *Making Sense of Chindia: Reflections on China and India*. New Delhi: India Research Press.

Statista. 2022. "Population of India from 1800 to 2020 (in Millions)". Retrieved on November 6, 2022 from www.statista.com/statistics/1066922/population-india-historical/.

United Nations Department of Economic and Social Affairs/Population Division. 2017. "World Population Prospects: The 2015 Revision, Volume I: Comprehensive Tables", pp. 18–21. Retrieved from https://esa.un.org/unpd/wpp/Publications/Files/WPP2015_Volume-I_Comprehensive-Tables.pdf.

United Nations Department of Economic and Social Affairs. 2019. "Population Size, Growth and Age Structure", in *World Population Prospects 2019. Highlights*. New York, NY: United Nations.

United Nations Department of Economic and Social Affairs. 2022a. " 'Ten Key Messages,' Global Population Growth and Sustainable Development". Retrieved on July 23, 2022 from www.un.org/development/desa/pd/sites/www.un.org.development.desa.pd/files/undesa_pd_2022_key_messages_global_population_growth.pdf.

United Nations Department of Economic and Social Affairs. 2022b. "World Population Policies 2021: Policy Related to Fertility". Retrieved from www.un.org/development/desa/pd/sites/www.un.org.development.desa.pd/files/files/documents/2022/May/undesa_pd_2022_key_messages_wpp_2021.pdf.

Wang, Gabe T. 1999. *China's Population: Problems, Thoughts and Policies*. Aldershot: Ashgate Publishing Limited.

Weeks, John R. 2016. *Population: An Introduction to Concepts and Issues*. Boston, MA: Cengage Learning.

World Bank. 2022. "GDP (Current US$) – All Countries and Economies". *The World Bank*. Retrieved on August, 11, 2022 from https://data.worldbank.org/indicator/NY.GDP.MKTP.CD?locations=IN&most_recent_value_desc=true.

Index

Note: Page numbers in *italics* indicate a figure and page numbers in **bold** indicate a table on the corresponding page.

For Product Safety Concerns and Information please contact our EU
representative GPSR@taylorandfrancis.com
Taylor & Francis Verlag GmbH, Kaufingerstraße 24, 80331 München, Germany

www.ingramcontent.com/pod-product-compliance
Ingram Content Group UK Ltd.
Pitfield, Milton Keynes, MK11 3LW, UK
UKHW020000200926
475702UK00015B/2402
* 9 7 8 1 0 3 2 3 0 9 5 5 2 *